Third Edition

PRINCIPLES
MICROECONOMICS
UNDERSTANDING OUR MATERIAL WORLD

Kendall Hunt
publishing company

Dave Shorow • Fred Newbury • Gus Herring

Kendall Hunt
publishing company

www.kendallhunt.com
Send all inquiries to:
4050 Westmark Drive
Dubuque, IA 52004-1840

Copyright © 2007, 2013, 2015 by Dave Shorow, Fred Newbury, and Gus Herring

ISBN 978-1-4652-7819-7

CONTENTS

What are the Principles of Economics for Living in a Material World?

Economics is resourcing: simply how we use our supply to gain maximum satisfaction. The process is an everyday experience. We know that an informed choice of using our resources will lead to the best outcomes. There are economic principles of resourcing that can help guide our decisions. Although each individual is given a different set of resources, resource principles apply to all allocations.

The Basic Assumptions and Goals of Economics: The Principles of Economics

1. We live in a material world where we seek more than just meeting our individual survival needs; we want more resources for health care, education, and safety for ourselves, our children, and our global community.

2. There are limits to our resource base. The world, as well as individuals, have a finite amount of resources available. Choices in resource use are limited by the amount of resources but also by economic opportunity cost. If an individual uses his/her resources for one opportunity, the same resources cannot be used for another opportunity. In order to make choices among resource alternatives, we must consider the short run economic costs versus the economic benefits as well as the longer term risks and uncertainties.

3. Goals of economic well-being are measured by both the quantity of goods and services and quality of life; neither is solely determining the other. As our basic needs are met, individuals seek to fill other needs and levels of fulfillment. More is not necessarily better. How we value our economic outcome is individually determined by our individual culture.

4. Individual achievement generally increases both personal and national income. Our economic choices are influenced by the macroeconomic environment. The environment, whether in an advanced or developing economy, does influence the individual choices. However, individual initiatives for a better life facilitate economic growth for both the individual and the nation. Market systems promote opportunity for economic achievement.

5. The macroeconomic environment is influenced by world economic conditions. Business fluctuations can be lessened or intensified by macroeconomic actions of consumers, business, and government.

6. Savings and Investment allocations are essential elements for individual and national progress. When income is saved and used for investment in capital goods to increase output or individually used for increased training/education, output is generally increased.

7. The current Global Market Economy is open to us both as suppliers and consumers. This material world market is connected and makes resources more available and competitive than at any other time. We as individuals have international opportunities to produce and sell or buy within the global material world.

Where Do We Begin Microeconomics?

Given these assumptions and goals of economic behavior, what is the pathway to understanding the principles of microeconomics? Each of us has a knowledge of the economy because of our individual (micro) experiences and we have a common goal of using our economic understanding to achieve greater economic well-being. Micro is distinguished from general economics. Microeconomics is often more detailed and even more methodical than the general world of economics. The tools and methods of microeconomics are more quantitative than macroeconomics and also less social/political in their context. The microeconomic analysis of business operations and consumerism are generally accepted and have remained constant over decades.

Microeconomics Course Overview

As we begin the course, we seek to understand the basic elements of terminology, history/culture, and capitalistic process with Lessons 1, 2, and 3 respectively. Whether we examine microeconomics or macroeconomics, the beginning elements are the same;

therefore, Lessons 1 through 2 are the same in our macro and micro courses. However, in Lesson 3 we include a transition to the specifics of microeconomics by applying supply and demand to economic growth. Lesson 4 is concerned primarily with market inefficiencies unlike the assumptions of efficient markets in Lesson 3. Lesson 5, 6, and 7 present the tools and measures of firm/consumer allocation. Lessons 8, 9, and 10 investigate the Theory of the Firm, analyzing firm allocation in varied organizational market forms from highly competitive to monopoly. Lesson 11 is a discussion of Factor Markets, supply-side elements and production options facing a firm. Lessons 12 and 13 discuss international markets and financial decisions facing a firm and a nation .

© Dave Allen Photography, 2013. Used under license from Shutterstock, Inc.

"The only thing potentially worse than not being able to see the forest for the trees is not being able to see the trees because of the forest."

–Anonymous

In microeconomics we seek to understand the formation and growth of consumer decisions and the responses by firms as in a tree of decision making compared to the macro forest. What is the basis of consumer decision making and how does this determine the environment of the total economy? Particular attention in the micro debate is the viability of the firm adapting to changes in consumer behaviors, worker and entrepreneurial needs, and technology. The landscape of the forest can change rapidly through the adaptive process of allocation by individual units. The process of allocation is determined by individuals making good choices within the resource process. Let's now consider the context of "making good choices."

Microeconomic Resourcing Process

The decision-making theme of economics is making good choices within a material world. Good choices are made by understanding these elements of allocation.

1. We are all constantly making resource allocation _choices_. Some choices are _small_, e.g. what to have for lunch … some are _bigger_, e.g. whether to study Economics tonight <u>or</u> use the time in some other way. Some _choices_ are _VERY_ big, e.g. what to choose for a college major. A reality is that _every choice_ we make is our attempt to obtain some type of _benefit_ (upside gain) either for ourselves or for someone else.

2. _Every choice_ that is made is <u>also</u> a person's attempt to _minimize_ (make as small as possible) the <u>following three realities on the "downside"</u>:

   a. _cost_ – in the <u>short</u> run what <u>must be _given up_</u> to obtain a "benefit" (this goes beyond just $$$),

   b. _uncertainty_ – in the <u>longer</u> run the amount of "benefit" <u>actually</u> obtained <u>may be _less_</u> than what was originally perceived,

   c. _risk_ – in the <u>longer</u> run the amount of "cost" <u>actually</u> paid <u>may be _more_</u> than what was originally perceived.

3. Both _uncertainty_ and _risk_ result from a "real world reality" called <u>limited information</u>. That is, whenever you have to make a really important _choice_, it seems like there is never enough <u>good</u> information available … at least <u>not at the moment</u> when you really need it.

4. Our choices are constantly being re-evaluated. Even a simple choice like having a cheeseburger for lunch can have additional "cost" an hour later if you did not initially have good information about the quality of the meat. In this example the *initial benefits* may have been what you perceived ... but the *additional cost* an hour later can turn out to be much greater.

5. The challenge in making a *good choice* is that in trying to increase the initial amount of a benefit there is usually an increase in short-run cost ... and often an increase in the longer-run *uncertainty* and risk. This means that we are all faced with another "real world reality" of having to make a *tradeoff* every time a *choice* is made. (Making a "tradeoff" means accepting additional cost, uncertainty, and risk in exchange for the possibility of additional benefit ... or accepting less benefit in exchange for less cost, uncertainty and risk.)

6. At a particular moment in time, regardless of whether you are in the role of a student, a consumer, a business person, a government official, or a member of a social or political group, there are *tradeoffs* that you have to make when trying to make a "good choice" that considers the longer run as well as the short run.

7. In summary ... a dynamic economy (and a dynamic society) can be viewed as *a CHAIN-REACTION of tradeoffs and choices* that are being made every day by millions of people. Our courses in *ECONOMICS* (including "intro," "macro," "micro," and "global") include a variety of learning experiences that will have one unified theme: "Trying to make the *good choices* (the good tradeoffs!) in a real world of constant challenges and on-going change."

Our course defines a journey through basic theory of making good decisions that largely defines the outcome of our economic well-being and that of our world.

The Principle of Microeconomic Analysis

An individual allocates his/her resources using economic reasoning comparing the costs of an action versus the benefits. This is called marginal analysis.

For the firm, the marginal benefits are related to profit while the marginal cost is the opportunity cost (cost compared to other opportunities using the same resources). If the net benefit of an investment choice is greater than the comparable resource allocations, then the opportunity exists for a positive resourcing.

The Principle of Microeconomics

Economic comprehension is the goal of studying economics. The fundamental rule of allocation throughout this course is applying the principle of marginal cost to marginal benefit. Good decisions are the result of basing a choice of allocation on this economic principle. A new action to allocate resources is only made if the new outcome is greater than the new cost. This same concept will be applied throughout Lessons 1-13 using different actions from consumer to global economic decisions. The pathway within the forest is based upon making good decisions applying this concept.

FUNDAMENTALS
OF A MARKET ECONOMY

INTRODUCTION

In this lesson, we will focus on some of the basic ideas that describe economics. As with any survey course, the learning objectives provide the basic foundation. Definitions, as well as an understanding of the methods used for analysis are also important components.

LEARNING OBJECTIVES

Please note the listed objectives. As you will see, the course materials are all objective driven.
This provides you with a constant way to direct and monitor your progress throughout the course.

1 OBJECTIVE ONE

Define economics. Describe how economists define human behavior. Why is this important in today's world?

2 OBJECTIVE TWO

Describe the difference between macroeconomics and microeconomics.

3 OBJECTIVE THREE

Describe the use of scientific approach to economics. What are tools and terms associated with scientific approach?

4 OBJECTIVE FOUR

Identify the goals of economics. Demonstrate an understanding of the related terms and concepts.

5 OBJECTIVE FIVE

Describe the difference between positive economics and normative economics.

I INTERACTIVE EXERCISE

Demonstrate an understanding of the basic circular flow model.

What is economics?

Economics inevitably involves some type of system—a system that is utilized to allocate resources. In more simple terms an economic system helps to determine "what is produced" and "who gets what."

Definition

While there are several elements to consider when attempting to define economics, the simplest definition focuses on economics as a study of the allocation of resources. Specifically, economics is the study of the choices, methods, and systems used by societies to allocate scarce resources.

"To allocate" our scarce resources (our productive assets) implies that we would like to divide them so they could be used in the best possible way. The idea that resources are "scarce" implies that we have limited amounts of these assets compared to our desire to have more of the things which those resources can produce. As individuals as well as a society, we continue to desire more—our wants seem to be insatiable (unable to be fully satisfied).

In short, then, the study of economics seeks to help us improve the choices, methods, and systems by which we allocate our scarce resources. In doing so we strive to better satisfy the basic needs (and hopefully some portion of the wants) that people have. We will study the behavior of the economy at the societal level as well as the economic behavior of individuals and organizations within our society.

Macro vs. micro

The discipline of economics is divided into two major areas of study: macroeconomics and microeconomics.

Macroeconomics is the study of the overall allocation of resources within a society; it is the study of the overall national economy. Macroeconomics analyzes how resources are used at the aggregate level (the total supply and demand for goods and services). This includes measures of performance such as the growth rate of the economy, inflation, unemployment, government expenditures, and total investment expenditures by business.

Microeconomics is the study of resource allocation from the perspective of smaller units in the economy such as the individual consumer and the individual business unit or firm. Microeconomics analyzes how resource allocation is influenced by consumers seeking "utility" (satisfaction of their needs and wants) and by businesses seeking "profits." Microeconomics includes measures of behavior and performance such as consumer utility patterns as well as business revenues, costs, and profits.

Both branches of economics seek to measure and analyze something called economic "efficiency."

An economic way of thinking

Economists are social scientists who try to measure the attainment of economic "efficiency." In concept, economic "efficiency" is maximized when the most utility is obtained for the most people. Economists, then, are social scientists who analyze the choices, methods, and systems that seek "efficiency" in the allocation of limited resources. There are a number of different realities and considerations that influence the quest for an "efficient" allocation of resources. These will be explored as we move through the course.

One of the skills required for economists is the ability to reason critically. Critical reasoning in economics is the ability to analyze the allocation process logically and evaluate the expected outcomes and uncertainties of various courses of action. Critical reasoning in economics is an activity which considers alternative courses of action and expected results relative to the costs and risks of each action.

The principles of economics are the generally accepted concepts and theories that relate to the overall allocation of resources. These principles are derived from the observation of human behaviors that occur over and over as people attempt to meet their material needs and wants. This body of knowledge does evolve as we develop an even better and deeper understanding of basic economic relationships.

Policy economics is the application of economic principles when a government is attempting to formulate an approach that will contribute to an efficient and growing economy, yet one that is also reasonably stable and equitable (fair). A strong insight into basic economic relationships is critical to understanding how the government attempts to manage parts of our economic system in trying to reach these objectives.

WHY STUDY ECONOMICS?

There are widely divergent reasons why people study economics, but for a student the answer is often very simple—it is a required subject or part of a core area of study. The most common reason for this requirement is to promote an understanding of how a society can best use its resources and how as a society we must make rational choices in seeking a better standard of living. In a free market society based on capitalism, an informed electorate is a necessity for social and economic development. A better understanding of our economic system is essential for all citizens in order for good choices to be made in our ongoing roles as business people, as consumers, as savers/investors, as taxpayers, and as voters. In all of these roles the critical reasoning skills mentioned earlier are extremely important.

ANALYTIC TOOLS

What Are the Tools of Economics?

Tool 1 - Rational Analysis:

The study of economics involves the use of a logical pattern of thinking as well as the use of a number of analytical tools. Economists assume that people make rational choices by being able to understand what they want and that people consider the benefits, the costs, the uncertainties, and the risks that are involved in a particular path of action.

Tool 2 - Marginal Analysis:

When studying different possible paths of action, the results of inputs versus outputs are considered. An application of this concept would be involved in making the choice of whether or not to go to another (or your first) country music concert this month. The marginal cost (the additional cost of an additional event) is considered relative to the marginal benefit (additional amount of satisfaction expected). When deciding whether or not to undertake the action, a rational person considers the marginal cost relative to the marginal benefit.

The benefit of an action then is simply the "utility" that the action creates (recall from a bit earlier in this lesson that "utility" is simply "satisfaction"). Total utility is the total amount of satisfaction gained from all allocations of resources while marginal utility is the additional amount of pleasure gained from the allocation of one additional unit of resource. Marginal utility in the example above is the benefit gained from going to the additional (or first) concert. The choice to attend one more concert this month is economically justified if the marginal benefit is greater than the marginal cost; that is, if the utility gained is greater than the utility which had to be given up. This leads us to a discussion of our next tool: opportunity cost analysis.

Tool 3 - Opportunity Cost Analysis:

Anytime we receive a benefit from the use of a resource, it comes at a cost because we could have used that resource for a different opportunity. All of our resource allocations come at a cost and this cost is compared to the benefit we receive in deciding if we should undertake the action. In the above illustration of going to a concert, an individual must certainly consider the monetary costs of going to the concert such as the ticket price and transportation, but one must also consider what had to be forgone (given up) in order to attend. Perhaps the person could have caught up on her/his sleep, or worked and made additional income. These opportunities are lost if the person chooses to attend the concert.

The overall cost of the choice to attend the additional concert includes not only the out-of-pocket costs, but also the opportunity cost (the lost sleep or the lost wages . . . whichever might have provided the greatest utility at the time). Every activity that we undertake requires us to not do other activities. The total cost of a choice is the out-of-pocket costs plus the opportunity cost (the most desirable alternative that was given up). The overall cost of this course includes the direct dollar expenditures plus the wages that you could have earned during the time allocated to the course.

Tool 4 - Variable Analysis:

In analysis of any situation, economists carefully consider the relationships among all of the interacting variables. But there is a special emphasis placed on considering changes in only one variable at a time. This is called "ceteris paribus" (Latin translated as meaning "with all other things the same").

Any one variable is evaluated for its impact on a situation rather than in combination with many other variables. This concept is illustrated when an economist seeks to find the main factor determining individual income in the United States.

There are many variables which determine how much income an individual is able to earn during his or her career, but a major variable is the level of education. Variable analysis reveals that college graduates as a group make considerably more income than high school graduates over the course of their careers. Once again, there are a number of variables involved in this type of study, but they must be considered one at a time. Economists use the "ceteris paribus" approach to help identify cause-and-effect relationships. It is important to note here that correlation between two variables (e.g., education and income) does not always mean that one variable is actually causing the other variable to change.

ECONOMIC GOALS

There are a number of different goals in our economy that are constantly being pursued. For example, one goal of the consumer is to maximize utility. One goal of the business firm is to maximize profit (this may or may not be accomplished by maximizing the consumer's utility). In the case of the business firm there are actually many participants whose goals must be recognized including workers, management, stockholders, bondholders, and even the government.

At the macroeconomic level, we strive to improve the allocation of resources in order to produce a better standard of living for everyone. The following are generally accepted national goals for our economy:

Macroeconomics Goals

Growth is the goal that seeks an increase in the amount of goods and services being produced. The amount of goods and services produced is measured as Gross Domestic Product (GDP). The goal is to increase the real value (value without inflation) of goods and services and to create new jobs in that growing economy.

Efficiency is the goal to produce a maximum output of the most desirable items with a given input of resources (more on this in Lesson Two).

Full employment is a goal strongly related to "growth" and seeks the full use of workers who are willing and able to be productive. Attainment of this goal is often reported on in media as the "unemployment rate." Since an unemployment rate of "0%" is not realistic (or desirable as we shall see later), the actual goal is to have a reasonably low level of unemployment in a growing economy with low inflation.

Stability is a constant concern as we attempt to achieve a balance between a low rate of inflation and a low rate of unemployment in a growing economy. This is an extremely important macro concept and will be discussed in much more detail.

Ecological balance emphasizes the need to maintain a sustainable global environment. Ecological balance assumes that the global economy can achieve its other economic goals while maintaining a healthy, living planet.

Freedom for citizens is a goal of economics within capitalism. The freedom to make purchases as desired and to work and live independent of extensive controls by government is a basic and fundamental principle of free markets and free people.

Social balance—we seek a reasonable balance within our social structure and between our public sector (local, state and federal government) and our private sector (households and business firms). A reasonable balance within the social structure and among the economic sectors requires responsible actions on the part of all participants.

Equity (or fairness) in the distribution of income is essential to the health and survival of a free society. It is important to note here that an "equitable" distribution of the economic pie does not mean an "equal" piece of pie for everybody. It does mean that every person should have a equal opportunity to *earn* a larger piece of the pie and that no person should be left to suffer in unreasonable poverty.

A **balance of trade** within the **international markets** is an increasingly important goal. Over time a nation must balance its position within the global markets in order to achieve and maintain prosperity.

Microeconomics Goals

Just as there are economic goals for the economy as a whole (macroeconomics), there are also goals for individual business firms and consumers. If you were starting a new business what microeconomic goals would you seek to fulfill?

One goal you may think of first would be profit. Profit is a fundamental reason for the existence of a firm, but there are many other goals to consider. The firm might start very small and you would seek its growth. When a firm begins to expand, you must consider the welfare of your employees, managers, stockholders, bondholders, and of course, consumers. In addition, your firm must satisfy government requirements and moral responsibilities that you believe are important.

Goals of Microeconomics for a Firm

- Profit
- Growth
- Consumer Satisfaction
- Employee, Manager, Stockholder, and Bondholder Interests
- Government and Moral Responsibilities

Goals of Microeconomics for Consumers

- Utility (consumer satisfaction)
- Value Added (additional benefit or marginal utility compared to price or marginal cost)

Debates in Economic Policy

The variation in the amount of emphasis placed on each of the goals above is determined by the cultural values of a society. It is a reality, however, that some goals will have to take priority over other goals. Although human nature desires maximum attainment of every goal, some of our goals are conflicting (as progress is attained on one, progress on the other may be sacrificed). Some goals are actually complementary (progress on one can be made at the same time as progress on the other).

Growth and full employment tend to be "complementary" goals while growth and stability tend to be "conflicting." When growth is strong, full employment is likely. But when growth is strong it is also likely (although not a certainty) that there will be inflation. If inflation does occur, that is definitely in conflict with the goal of stability.

Vigorous debates are likely when macroeconomic goals and changes in government policy are discussed. There is much agreement among economists about the basic principles (generalizations) about how an economy "works." There is, however, considerable disagreement about which goals should be emphasized, how to pursue these goals, and how much emphasis should be given to government policy. An understanding of the possible roles that the government sector might play (in relation to the private sector and the foreign sector) is critical in developing an overall understanding of our material world.

The two macroeconomic goals that tend to be emphasized the most by the government sector are stability (trying to keep both unemployment and inflation low) and equity. The two goals that tend to be emphasized the most in the private sector by microeconomic actions are efficiency and growth. At this point it is very important to understand that there will be "tradeoffs" when attempts are made toward progress on any of these four goals. This means that gains in stability or equity will often lead to short-run, or possibly long-run, losses in growth or efficiency and vice versa. Even within the goal of stability, an improvement in the unemployment rate can in the longer run result in a worse inflation rate and, once again, vice versa. The ongoing challenge in any society is to understand the reality of "tradeoffs" and then try to make good choices that lead to a reasonable balance in the attainment of its economic goals.

POSITIVE VS. NORMATIVE ECONOMICS

Positive economics is the description of an economy by stating facts or objective data. The inflation rate or unemployment rate as measured by a government agency would be considered an example of positive economics. If we say, "the current unemployment rate is 5%" it would be positive economics because it is a statement of fact—no opinion is stated or implied.

Normative economics is the statement of an opinion about the economy. It is a subjective view. Normative economics describes many of the disagreements among economists relating to what goals should be emphasized or what the economic policies of the government should be. If we say, "the unemployment rate has not risen above 5% because of the government's aggressive fiscal policy," that is quite different from simply stating, "The current unemployment rate is 5%." Now we see that an opinion has been expressed and, yes, the "scientific testing" of opinions and theories opens additional areas for discussion and disagreement.

Debates within economics are expected to be rationally based upon widely accepted economic principles and well-tested (or at least testable) theories. As we consider the scientific testing (and real world application) of economic theories, we will see how much "normative economics" can enter into the debates about which government policies should be used. Biased opinions without any probable economic merit can be very destructive. Societies without bias in their economic debates appear to make better choices about how to efficiently utilize their resources.

Another difficulty that sometimes occurs within economic debates is called the fallacy of composition. A fallacy of composition exists when we conclude that something that is beneficial for an individual person or an individual business is also beneficial for society as whole. An example of this concept would be if you concluded that your pollution of the creek behind your house or business is beneficial since it saves you the hassle of hauling your trash to the dump. What if all of the people along the creek (including those "upstream" from your place) do what is "beneficial" for each of them individually? What is beneficial for each person individually is not necessarily beneficial for society as a whole.

> ## Positive vs. Normative
> **Positive statements** assert facts and objective data.
>
> **Normative statements** assert how things ought to be.

THE CIRCULAR FLOW MODEL OF ECONOMICS

The **circular flow model** is used in our course to illustrate the basic relationships that exist between the household sector and business sector in a market-based economy. The government sector (whose responsibilities include developing policies to deal with the pollution problem mentioned above) will be added to the model in a later lesson along with the foreign sector.

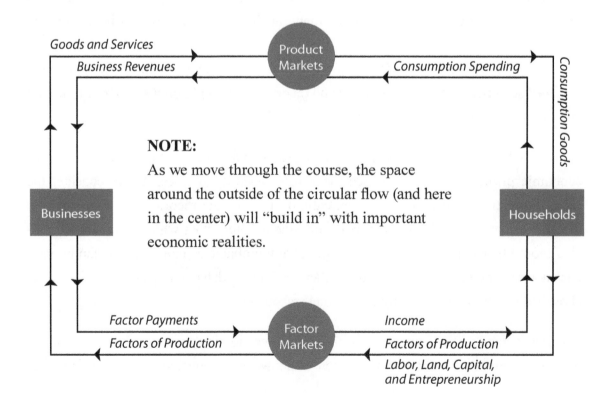

NOTE:
As we move through the course, the space around the outside of the circular flow (and here in the center) will "build in" with important economic realities.

In a market-based system the household sector usually owns the four basic economic resources. In concept the land, labor, capital, and entrepreneurship are provided to the business sector in exchange for the products and services produced by the business sector. This exchange is facilitated by two markets—the product market and the factor market.

In the factor (or resource market) located on the underside of the model, the households supply the land, labor, capital, and entrepreneurship to the businesses in exchange for four different types of income. Landholders (the owners of natural resource) receive rent. Labor (the owners of productive time and talent) receives wages. Capital holders (the owners of productive tools and equipment) receive interest. Entrepreneurs (the owners of business building skills) receive profits.

The **product market** is the exchange located on the topside of the circular flow. Businesses supply the goods and services, which are desired by the households. In turn the households pay for the goods and services with the income which they have received from the businesses. These payments become revenues for the businesses, which, in turn, they use to make the factor payments to the households. Yes, it is very much a circular flow.

Where is the actual starting point of this circular flow? In a market-based economy the answer is that it starts with the entrepreneur. It is the entrepreneur who has a new idea and takes the risk to start a business. The entrepreneur then employs some combination of the other three resources from the factor market to create a good or service and then tries to sell that item in the product market. If the entrepreneur is successful, then the circular flow will continue and will grow; otherwise the circular flow will cease (at least for that particular entrepreneur in that particular business).

The circular flow model is one of the most important concepts in all of economics. It provides an improved understanding of the microeconomic foundations of our society and it provides important insights into many of our macroeconomic problems, such as recession and inflation.

Pay very close attention to the Circular Flow examples in the "Animations & Interactives" component of the course. In each new lesson important "economic realities" will be added to this model.

REAL WORLD ECONOMICS

IS A COLLEGE DEGREE WORTH THE COST?

For many years the answer to this question was an automatic "yes." However, with rapidly rising costs in higher education (tuition at some private schools is more than $30,000 per year) that question has been receiving closer attention. Is a college degree really worth the dollar cost and the opportunity cost? Is the marginal (extra) benefit greater than the marginal (extra) cost?

According to ongoing research by the College Board, the answer is still yes—especially when you look at the lifetime earnings of a high school graduate as compared to someone with a bachelor's degree. The college graduate will earn (on average) 60% more that those with a high school diploma. Over a lifetime, that amounts to over $800,000. It certainly appears that the marginal benefit is still greater than the marginal cost—which makes it a sound decision.

Economics is the study of the choices, methods, and systems used by societies to allocate scarce resources.

Fallacy of composition exists when we conclude that something that is appropriate for an individual must be also appropriate for society. Example: If it is good for the individual to save more, it must be good for the overall economy.

Macroeconomics is a study of the allocation of resources relative to the overall national economy or large sectors within it.

Marginal Analysis is the comparison of the marginal (extra) costs to the marginal (extra) benefits used as an aid in decision-making. Example: Is the extra (marginal) benefit of a college degree greater than the marginal cost?

Microeconomics is a study of the allocation of resources in smaller units, specifically the individual consumer and the individual business unit or firm.

Normative Economics is the description of the economy where opinion is utilized and value judgments are made. Example: because of government's effective use of fiscal policy, the unemployment rate has fallen to only 5%.

Opportunity Cost Analysis is the examination of the cost of a different opportunity that must be forgone in order to pursue a benefit from selected use of a resource. All of our decisions come at a cost, and this cost is compared to the benefit we receive in deciding if we should undertake the action.

Positive Economics is the description of an economy by stating facts or using specific data. No opinion is involved. Example: The unemployment rate is 5%.

Policy Economics is the application of the principles of economics to government policy actions. Government seeks to understand economic activities in order to influence economic activity.

Rational Analysis is the study of economics using a logical pattern of thinking as well as analytical tools for analysis.

Variable Analysis is a key characteristic of quantitative research. Economists consider the variable relationships in their analysis with an emphasis on considering the relationship of one variable at a time. This is called *ceteris paribus* (Latin translated as meaning one at a time). Each variable is evaluated relative to itself rather than in combination with many other variables.

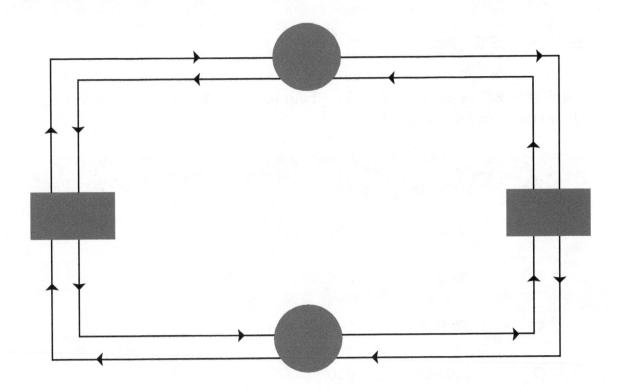

EXERCISE 1 :

A: Complete the circular flow chart above.

B: The exchange flows in the top of the model are called the _____ market.

The exchange flows in the bottom of the model are called the _____ market.

APPLIED EXERCISES

EXERCISE 2:

Consider each of the following costs and benefits and find the marginal cost and marginal benefit of each. These projects must be undertaken in order from A to D. Otherwise the marginal figures become confusing.

Project	Cost	Benefit	Marginal Cost	Marginal Benefit
A	$1,000	100		
B	$2,000	300		
C	$5,000	500		
D	$10,000	650		

EXERCISE 3:

Consider the cost of each of the vacations and explain whether or not you should undertake each. If you have $1,250 to spend, how should you allocate your funds and why?

	Cost	Benefit	Action
Vacation A	$500	$1,400	
Vacation B	$1,000	$3,250	
Vacation C	$750	$2,300	
Vacation D	$1,250	$3,750	

APPLIED EXERCISES

EXERCISE 4 :

Describe whether each economic statement applies to a macroeconomic or a micro-economic topic.

A: Corn prices continue to rise throughout U.S. markets.

B: The level of U.S. inflation continues to fall.

C: The unemployment rate has increased according to the Department of Labor.

D: The price of automobiles fell last quarter.

E: Government spending has increased again this month according to new data.

F: Employment is beginning to increase.

G: The demand for used cars has increased.

H: Oil company profits rose last quarter.

EXERCISE 1 :

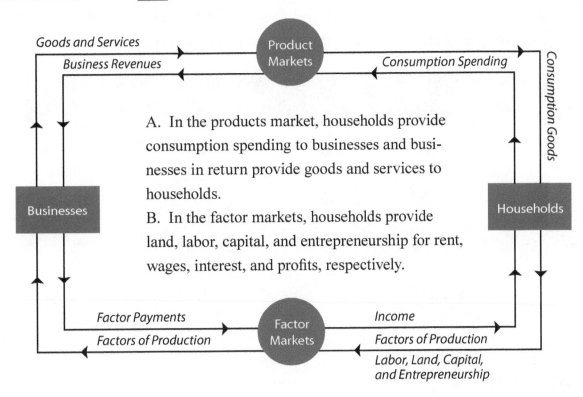

Goods and Services

Business Revenues

Product Markets

Consumption Spending

Consumption Goods

A. In the products market, households provide consumption spending to businesses and businesses in return provide goods and services to households.

B. In the factor markets, households provide land, labor, capital, and entrepreneurship for rent, wages, interest, and profits, respectively.

Businesses

Households

Factor Payments

Factors of Production

Factor Markets

Income

Factors of Production

Labor, Land, Capital, and Entrepreneurship

EXERCISE **2** :

Consider each of the following costs and benefits and find the marginal cost and marginal benefit of each. Must be undertaken in order from A to D.

PROJECT	COST	BENEFIT	MARGINAL COST	MARGINAL BENEFIT
A	$1,000	100	$1,000	100
B	$2,000	300	$1,000	200
C	$5,000	500	$3,000	200
D	$10,000	650	$5,000	150

EXERCISE **3** :

The largest benefit from spending $1,250 would be Vacation D because no other combination is within the income limits and provides more benefits

EXERCISE 4 :

Describe whether each economic statement applies to a macroeconomic or a micro-economic topic.

A. Micro - Corn prices continue to rise throughout U.S. Markets.

B. Macro - The level of U.S. inflation continues to fall.

C. Macro - The unemployment rate has increased according to the Department of Labor.

D. Micro - The price of automobiles fell last quarter.

E. Macro - Government spending has increased again this month according to new data.

F. Macro - Employment is beginning to increase.

G. Micro - The demand for used cars has increased.

H. Micro - Oil company profits rose last quarter.

THE
ECONOMIC PROBLEM

INTRODUCTION

In this lesson, we will focus on some of the basic
ideas that describe the **economic problem** and the
beginnings of a market economy. As with any survey
course, the objectives provide the basic foundations.
The questions posed by the economic problem give
rise to the need for a system that will help to allocate
scarce resources.

LEARNING OBJECTIVES

Please note the listed objectives. As you will see, the course materials are all objective driven.
This provides you with a constant way to direct and monitor your progress throughout the course.

1 OBJECTIVE ONE

Define the economic problem and describe the three economic systems that have been employed throughout history to address this problem.

2 OBJECTIVE TWO

Identify the four basic economic questions that every economic system must answer.

3 OBJECTIVE THREE

Identify the four basic economic resources (the factors of production) that every economic system has available to help answer those four basic economic questions.

4 OBJECTIVE FOUR

Describe the historical evolution of the market system and describe the contributions of five prominent economists to this evolution.

5 OBJECTIVE FIVE

Use the production possibilities model to explain the economic problem and the related concepts of efficiency, equity, stability and growth.

I INTERACTIVE EXERCISE

Use the production possibilities model to explain tradeoffs and opportunity cost.

THE ECONOMIC PROBLEM?

The economic problem is an idea that is very basic to our study. The problem centers on the contrast between unlimited human wants and the relative scarcity of all resources. The questions posed by this problem give rise to the need for a system that will help to allocate scarce resources.

There are two parts to the economic problem—first, human wants are insatiable (unable to be fully satisfied). As a group humans desire to have more goods and services than are available. This tends to be a natural state of the human condition. We always seem to want more. Second, resources are limited in nature—resources are finite. There are fixed amounts of resources available at any one time and these resources can only be directed toward satisfying a limited number of human wants. The conclusion is that, taken as a whole, our wants exceed our limited resources. Therein lies the nature of the economic problem.

While the economic problem is as old as society itself, the systems developed to answer the economic problem are relatively new. Macroeconomics has become a study of these large systems while microeconomics has become a study of business behavior and consumer behavior within these systems. Overall then economics is the study of how these behaviors and systems interact to allocate scarce resources toward the satisfaction of unlimited wants.

The economic problem focuses our attention on the efficient use of our scarce resources. Economic efficiency is gaining the most output to maximize consumer utility (or satisfaction) from a given amount of inputs. Productive efficiency is simply gaining the most output of certain items with a given amount of inputs, but not relating that output to consumer utility. A maximum of output of certain items, even if efficiently produced, is not desirable if consumers do not really want the items produced. Throughout history however, the goal of some powerful entities has been to emphasize the production of certain items regardless of whether or not those particular items were actually "wanted" by the citizens in that society. Do any examples come to mind? Perhaps pyramids or missiles or "the Edsel" (try that in a search engine) would be examples? But we should be careful to consider these examples (and any others) in the context of their time and culture.

ALLOCATION

There are four questions of allocation that must be addressed by any economic system in striving for economic efficiency and responding to the economic problem.

The Four Questions of Allocation

What to Produce?

We must determine what specific items will be produced and how much to produce of each item. Within a market-based system the process of responding to these questions is driven by consumers. Market-based systems are driven by consumer wants.

How to Produce?

In a market-based system this question is answered primarily by businesses. In trying to produce what consumers want, an individual firm will try to use the most efficient combination of resources. This approach keeps the firm's production costs down and its profits up.

Who to Produce For?

This is the question of how the items will be distributed among the population or what approach to "income distribution" is considered fair and equitable. This question is largely answered in a market economy by individual productivity. Individuals who produce the largest quantities of those items which are considered most desirable will be rewarded with the highest income. This raises several interesting issues which will be addressed as we proceed through the course.

How do Economic Systems Adapt?

The fourth question of economic allocation is answered in a market economy by competition. The goal of efficiency is to produce the maximum output of desirable items with a given input. For a business this will lead to a gain in market share which, in turn, creates market power. Every modern society has choices in how resources are allocated. But cultural values still have a very strong influence in determining this allocation process. Pay close attention to the "market mechanisms" as presented in the PowerPoint section.

The Standard of Living

The standard of living in a society is ultimately determined by the amount of resources that are available and how efficiently they are used. There is a complex economic process involved in determining what is produced as well as how much of each item is produced (and whether it is produced by national or international sources). This economic process begins with the four factors of production.

Factors of Production

The factors of production are simply the four basic categories of economic resources used for creating goods and services.

FIGURE 2.1

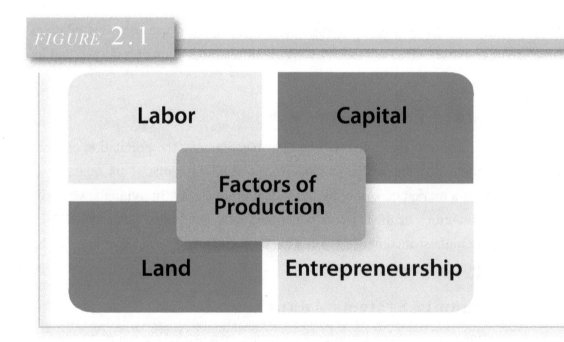

Land

The first factor of production is land. In order to produce and deliver any economic good or service there must be some use of natural resources. The basic economic term encompassing all natural resources is—"Land." Regardless of whether the item is wheat or the World Wide Web (or anything in between), "land" will be a necessary factor of production. It is obvious that wheat production requires "dirt" but after a moment's thought it is equally apparent that services delivered over "the Web" require such basic natural resources as silicon (for computer chips), coal (to generate the electricity) and even air (to carry the waves of wireless information).

Labor

The second factor of production is labor. All production involves some amount of human effort. The time and talent of humans (labor) must be mixed with the other factors of production in order for goods and services to be created. Labor is a very highly valued factor of production since it is very closely tied to increasing a society's standard of living. The efficiency and effectiveness of labor are determined by peoples' skill and knowledge as well as their attitude and their use of economic capital.

Capital

The third factor of production is capital. The term economic (or "real") capital describes the tools, facilities and equipment that aid in the production of all products and services. In this sense the term "capital" is not money but rather is used to describe the man-made tools used in the production process. The term "capital" includes computers and office buildings as well as shovels and dump trucks. Capital, then, describes any tool that aids in production—regardless of how simple or complex. Capital is also referred to as the "manufactured resource" and must be created by human effort before it, in turn, can be used to create other products.

We normally use the term financial capital (or business investment) to describe the money used to purchase the "real" (or economic) capital. The funds for business investment must come from corporate earnings that are retained for that purpose or from household savings that are borrowed by businesses. Business investment is critical for economic growth. Investment by businesses with better economic capital means that our productive capacity, and our economy, will have greater efficiency as well as increased opportunities for growth in the future.

Entrepreneurial Skill

The fourth factor of production is entrepreneurial skill. Entrepreneurial skill is the ability of a person: 1) to conceive a business idea (to innovate), 2) to take the risk involved in implementing the idea, and 3) to bring together the other three resources in an efficient combination. Entrepreneurial skill tends to be the most highly valued resource in a market-based economy. Entrepreneurs are well compensated with profits if they provide high utility to consumers at a relatively low cost. While land, labor and capital are utilized by all economic systems, the entrepreneur is unique to the market-based economy.

HISTORY

The history of economics describes how the basis for choice has changed over time with different allocation systems. This has been an evolutionary process and has followed changing social and political values as well as technological innovation. The human response to the economic problem (limited resources and unlimited wants) has, over time, produced three basic types of economic systems.

Tradition

The first system was tradition. In a traditional economic system the basic resources were allocated by the customs and folkways long used by a particular society or culture. These systems were often primitive, but also provided relative stability for that society. A difficulty with this approach was that any type of suggested change or improvement was often met with strong resistance.

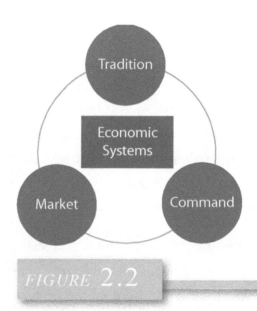

FIGURE 2.2

Command

The second system is a command (or authority) system which involves a strong central government or leader making all decisions relative to resource allocation. This system is controlled by only a few people who make all of the fundamental economic choices for that society. Command systems allow for very little, if any, private ownership of resources.

Market

The third system is the market. Within this system, producers and consumers interact to determine the allocation of the four basic resources. What is produced and how much is produced of each item is determined by market supply and market demand. The market allows for the free interaction of buyers and sellers and also provides for the private ownership of most resources.

The transition away from traditional and command systems gained momentum as the manor life of medieval Europe yielded in the 17th and 18th centuries to the beginning of the Industrial Revolution. This was a gradual process as economic markets evolved and adapted to new technologies and the need for different types of skilled labor. Not only was the economic system changing but the very nature of society itself, for better and for worse, was being changed forever.

The direct underpinning of today's modern market-based economic system can be found in 18th-century Britain. The prevailing philosophy of the time was logical order and natural law. An idea was taking shape that states of nature such as the standard of living could be logically explained and enhanced by applying several fundamental laws of economics. The condition of resource allocation was first considered in a comprehensive manner by Adam Smith.

The Father of Economics

Adam Smith, remembered as the "Father of Economics," was actually a professor of moral philosophy in Scotland. His best known work, *An Inquiry into the Nature and Causes of the Wealth of Nations*, was published in 1776 and provided the theoretical foundation of free-market economics. Within this text a number of economic issues were addressed. The most basic question in economics regarding "what to produce" was answered by "consumer sovereignty." For Adam Smith the answer was clear—the demands of consumers should direct the supply processes of producers.

In *The Wealth of Nations* (the book's popular title) the question of how income and wealth should be distributed was answered by **productivity:** the volume and utility of a worker's output. The more "**utility**" that an individual created for society, the greater was the income and wealth to which that person was entitled. The overall market process was called the "invisible hand" and this is a phrase we often use to describe the benefits of competition within the market. The final element discussed by Smith was a **laissez faire** role for government. He explained that the purpose of government was to facilitate the market and, thereby, the government should have a very **limited role** in an efficient market system.

The Worldly Philosophers

Beginning with Adam Smith, the "worldly philosophers" of 18th and 19th century economics held widely varied but influential views on markets and governments. David Ricardo was an economist of note in the early 1800s. During his career in the London stock market, he shared many of Smith's views and also advocated a free and open economy, unencumbered by government restrictions. His most significant theory was comparative advantage, which argued that a nation will gain through trade by specializing in the good which it produces most efficiently. According to this theory a nation will gain from trade by specializing in that product where its opportunity costs are lowest.

After Ricardo's writings, Thomas Malthus became well known for his economic views that population grew geometrically (i.e., 2, 4, 8, 16) while food production grew only arithmetically (i.e., 1, 2, 3, 4). Thus, he predicted that economic activity would evolve in cycles of misery and catastrophe. His theory did not take into account advancements in technology or in the economic systems themselves, but his theory did suggest that there were some limits to economic growth.

Robert Owen, a successful industrialist of this period also had influence on the prevailing economic perspectives in England. The world of economics was in the romantic period of history, which argued that industrialization had many negative consequences and a more society-based system (less centered on the individual) would be better for everyone. Owen was a Welsh utopian socialist who believed that socialism was a remedy for the poverty of the period.

He viewed social systems as primary in determining economic activity and demanded that technology be subordinated to human interests through government intervention.

Another economic philosopher of the period was Karl Marx. Within his *Communist Manifesto*, published in 1848, he argued that capitalism itself would lead to socialism and then to communism as armies of unemployed workers would force economic change and a complete takeover of the economic system by the government. Marxian economics led to the creation of the communist state in Russia and influenced many other parts of the world. Marx was a prolific writer and had a profound impact on political and social systems in the 19th and 20th centuries.

Since the United States is considerably younger that the countries in Europe, it did not follow exactly the same economic evolution but these theories did impact the development of the United States. The classical economic views of Smith and Ricardo had considerable impact as the market economy began to grow in this country.

A Brief History of the American Economy

Financial as well as economic capital was secured from Europe to advance the American economy as it began to grow and prosper and we moved into the 1800s. Railroads became instrumental in bringing American businesses together. But this era also marked the beginning of a concentration of economic power in several sectors of the economy which included railroads, steel, and banking. The Sherman Anti-Trust Act was passed in 1890 to restrain the monopoly power which had been created in these economic sectors. This legislation was, in fact, designed to return competition to these markets.

During the early 1900s labor unions became an economic force. Workers demanded recognition of their fundamental role in the process of economic growth. Natural resources were abundant but in order to gain output, increasing numbers of workers were necessary.

The living standard of workers was very low at this time and many began to question the distribution of income within the economy. Workers formed unions to constitute a force within the system. After much strife unions were eventually recognized as legal entities having the right to collective bargaining.

The depression of the 1930s caused many people to lose confidence in what had become known as the "classical theories" of economics. As unemployment increased, a new theory was emerging. The new theory was from John M. Keynes and unfolded during the 1930s and 1940s. This Keynesian approach became widely accepted in the 1950s and 1960s only to be challenged in the 1970s by the monetarist theory and other related new classical theories.

The change in social attitudes that emerged in the 1960s with emphasis on greater equality of opportunity and income resulted in much conflict with traditional values. During this same period the Vietnam War added to the social turmoil.

Since the onset of the Industrial Revolution, accelerating change has been one of the major characteristics of our world. But our economic, political, and social systems have evolved and have responded to many challenges over these years. Change has been the only constant in this evolution and it will, undoubtedly, continue.

As you can see from the historical material outlined above, economic theories have evolved substantially since the 1770s. One of the challenges in modern economics is to describe in simple terms the sometimes complex human choices that we encounter in today's world. During this course we will examine several different "models" (pictures of economic behavior and human choices) that will provide very important insights.

THE PRODUCTION POSSIBILITIES MODEL

The "PPM" (or "PPF"—Production Possibilities Frontier) illustrates the maximum potential output of a society at a point in time. Because there are many different variables that affect economic output, we need to note the three simplifying assumptions that are used with this model. Initially we will assume that: 1) the society produces only two goods and these are graphed in various combinations using the x- and y- axes; 2) the factors of production remain constant in time and are fully utilized; 3) technology remains constant in time and is fully utilized. The resulting concave curve describes the various output combinations that are possible and this curve is labeled as the Production Frontier. By producing at any point on the curve, maximum output or *production efficiency* is obtained. Recall that *economic efficiency* requires the production of that one specific output which consumers find most desirable.

FIGURE 2.3

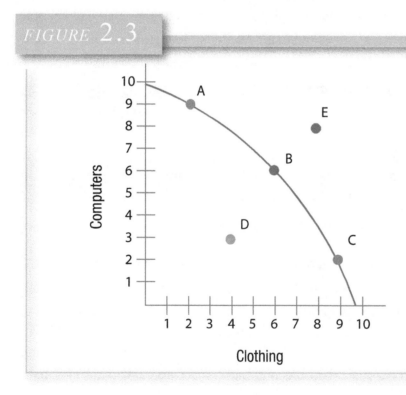

Point D: Any point inside the frontier (curve) describes an economy with unemployment of resources or underemployment of resources. Underemployment occurs when a resource is not efficiently and fully utilized. This occurs when a worker (labor) is not able to work at his highest skill level or when a manufacturing plant (capital) is only being utilized at a portion of its capacity. Unemployment occurs when some resources are totally unused, such as some workers being unable to find any job at all or some manufacturing plants that are being totally shut down.

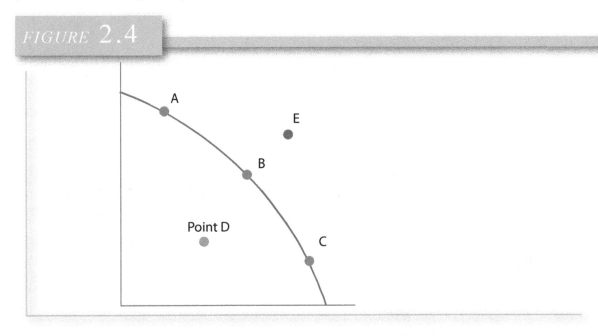

FIGURE 2.4

Point E: Any point that is outside the frontier (curve) describes an economy in which the resources are unattainable with current technology and current available resources.

FIGURE 2.5

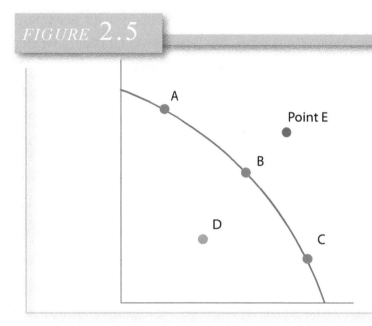

Frontier Shift: This represents an overall increase (or decrease) in the potential amount of output. When the entire curve shifts outward (or inward), this would indicate that either the amounts of resources available have increased (or decreased) or that the level of technology has changed. The widespread business use of Internet technology has certainly moved the production frontier outward. In times past the increased availability of oil (a "land" resource) moved the frontier outward. Certainly the destruction of a country's productive resources in a time of war or widespread natural disaster moves the frontier inward in a very dramatic way.

FIGURE 2.6

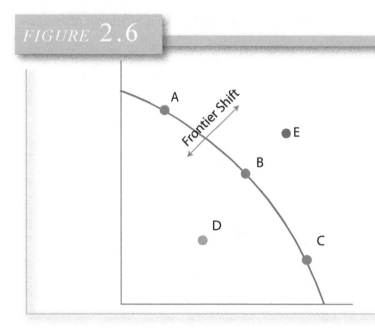

Growth: For the long run it is important to focus on the idea of an outward shift in the frontier. Growth in the production possibilities curve is possible when we loosen our assumptions about resources and technology always being fixed. Increases in technology and increases in the availability of resources are both possible over time if people have the incentive to be creative. If either one or some combination of these increases can be encouraged in a society, a better standard of living and improved quality of life can be shared by all.

FIGURE 2.7

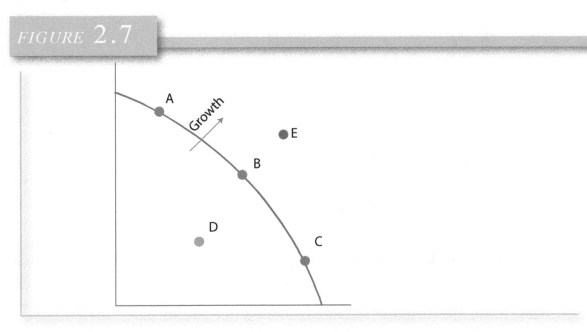

The production possibilities curve may decrease or shift left with a decrease in available resources. When forces of nature decrease resources, the frontier will decrease.

FIGURE 2.8

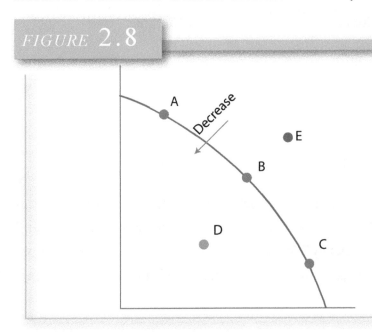

FIGURE 2.9

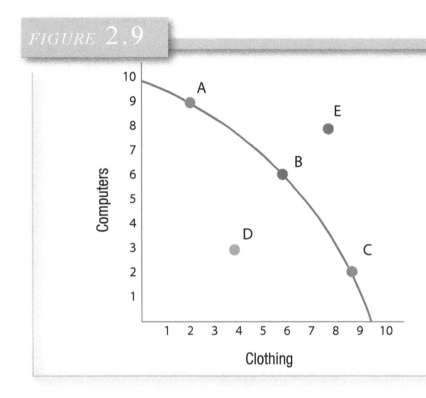

Once again we note that the points in the graph are labeled A through E. All of these points are very important to understand. By reviewing the numerical values at each point (by going horizontally across from each point as well as down to find the numerical values), one can better understand the basic production possibilities concepts. We will be using these production possibilities concepts in each and every lesson throughout the course.

Point	Computers	Units of Clothing
A	9	2
B	6	6
C	2	9
D	3	4
E	8	8

Point B represents the production of six computers in combination with six units of clothing. Since Point B is on the frontier that represents an economy that has "full employment" and "production efficiency." We do not, however, have enough information to know if this point represents "allocative efficiency" and, therefore, "economic efficiency" for this society.

Point D represents the production of only three computers in combination with only four units of clothing. This represents an unemployment or underemployment situation within the model (note that Point D lies inside the frontier).

Point E represents the production of eight computers in combination with eight units of clothing. This represents an unattainable situation (note that Point E lies outside the frontier).

Now let's explore the two other points (A and C) that are actually on the frontier along with Point B. All three points (A, B, and C) represent "full employment" and "production efficiency" (since they are all on the frontier). Question: What is the **benefit** and what is the **cost** of moving from Point B to Point C?

The "benefit" and the "cost" of moving from Point B to Point C are found by taking the numerical values at B and subtracting those from the values at C. At Point B there are six units of clothing produced along with six computers. At Point C there are nine units of clothing produced, but only two computers. In a nutshell then, to have the benefit of three more units of clothing (9 minus 6), there would be a cost of four computers (2 minus 6). Four computers would be "given up" to obtain three units of clothing if this society moved from Point B to Point C.

Would the move described above from Point B to Point C be a good choice for this society? This is a bit deeper question than we can fully explore in this lesson. This goes to the question of allocative and economic efficiency for this society and the utility of clothing versus the utility of computers at this moment in time and in the future. Just to take a very quick look at the issue, here are a couple of questions: 1) What if it is very cold outside at the moment and there is no electricity? Would Point B be a better choice for this society than Point C? 2) What if we have plenty of electricity and no real need for extra clothing at the moment, but in the future we would like a better variety of both clothing and computers? Would Point A be an even better choice for the future than either Point B or Point C? At Point A perhaps we could even "export" those two units of clothing and "import" some food from the country next door? These kinds of questions about benefits, costs, and "allocative efficiency" (present and future) might be explored further in a discussion board or perhaps in a classroom discussion.

Opportunity cost in the PPF

The basic opportunity cost of a choice is illustrated by a movement from one point on the PPF curve to another point on the curve (as we introduced in the discussion just above). To determine the basic "cost" of the change (as well as the basic "benefit") we must examine the coordinates of the points on each axis to find the amount of gain and loss from the former position. If the cost from one position to another is the same (constant), then the graphical relationship is a straight line and is referred to as constant cost.

In order to gain more of one, more units of the other must be sacrificed, then there is an increasing cost relationship. Increasing costs are present when resources are not perfectly shiftable; when resources are not as good at producing one thing as they are at producing the other. This is usually the case in most "real world" situations. We must also keep in mind the reality that one unit of clothing at a certain point in time may or may not be more highly desired in the society than one computer.

For another example of the "increasing cost" concept, let's consider a situation where a nation can produce both wine and beef. However, in order to produce more wine beyond some point the nation must give up larger and larger amounts of beef output. Land used for beef production is usually not equally well suited for wine production. If another equivalent increase in wine production is desired, then even more land will need to be taken from beef production than in the last round of resource shifting. This would be just to obtain the same increase in wine output as we obtained with the previous resource shift.

In summary, if a nation's goal was to increase wine output, the nation would typically have to sacrifice more and more of its beef production. This is because the land resource is not equally suited for the production of both products. Can you think of a similar example for the labor resource? What if (following up on an example from Lesson One) we wanted to increase the output of country music concerts? Or the output of professional sports entertainment? Are we all equally well talented to produce "an equivalent level" of those entertainment services? Some of us are probably not perfectly "shiftable resources" in those examples.

The production possibilities model is a very important tool and one that you will see again and again as we move through the course. The PPM introduces a graphical method of analysis and emphasizes the two realities that are an inescapable part of economics—scarcity necessitates choice and every choice has a cost. If scarcity did not exist and we did not have to make choices that have costs, then we would have no real need for economics.

Authority or Command System is an economic system controlled by a central authority that owns and allocates resources.

Capital: The manufactured resource is the combination of tools and equipment that aid in production.

Economic Efficiency is the act of gaining the most output to maximize consumer utility with a given amount of input.

The Economic Problem is the contrast between virtually unlimited human wants and the limited availability of resources.

Entrepreneurial Skill is the entity in a market economy that combines land, labor, and capital into a finished product or service.

Factors of Production are the basic economic resources that are required in production—land, labor, capital, and entrepreneurial skill.

Insatiable is a human condition where wants are incapable of complete satisfaction.

Labor: The huma resource is the whole of human physical and mental effort required to produce any product.

Land is a primary natural resource required to produce any product.

Market Economy is a system that allows free interaction between buyer and seller in the market place. It is characterized by private ownership of resources.

Opportunity Cost: Due to scarcity, the choice of one product means giving up something else. Opportunity cost is the alternative not chosen.

Production Possibilities Curve is a model that shows the tradeoff that exists between two goods or services that could potentially be produced by a full-employment, full-output economy assuming that all resources are fixed.

Traditional Economic System is a system that allows prevailing customs to determine the allocation of resources.

EXERCISE **1** :PRODUCTION POSSIBILITIES TABLE

Types of Production	Product Alternatives				
	A	B	C	D	E
Computers (millions)	0	2	4	6	10
Cell Phones (millions)	30	27	21	12	0

A: What do the points indicate? How does the table reflect the law of increasing opportunity costs? Explain. If the economy is currently at Point C, what is the cost of 2 million more computers in terms cell phones? Of 6 million more cell phones in terms of computers?

B: Upon what specific assumptions is the production possibilities curve based?

EXERCISE 2 : PRODUCTION POSSIBILITIES CURVE

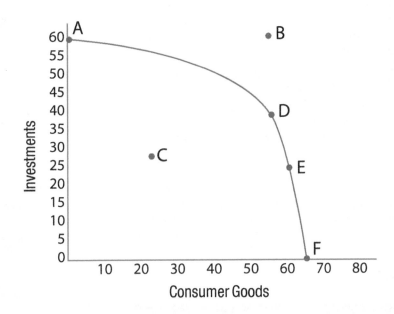

A: Describe the economic implications of Points A–F?

B: Upon what specific assumptions is the production possibilities curve based?

C: Which allocations will lead to greater future growth?

EXERCISE 3 :

Assume you are an owner of a small firm that employs two workers at a cost of $100 in wages each and who each produce two widgets per day, and you can sell each widget for $75. Assume employee costs are your only cost. Should you hire a third worker who can make one widget per day and whose wage is $60, but now the selling price will drop to $60 each as you can sell five rather than four widgets?

EXERCISE 1 :

A. What do the points on the curve indicate? How does the curve reflect the law of increasing opportunity costs? Explain. If the economy is currently at Point C, what is the cost of 2 million more computers in terms cell phones? Of 6 million more cell phones in terms of computers?

The points on the matrix illustrate the tradeoff between computers and cell phones. The law of increasing costs is present because as more of either product is produced from Point C, the costs increase. From Point C, the cost of 2 million more computers is 9 million cell phones that have to be given up. From Point C, the cost of 6 million more cell phones is 2 million computers.

B. Upon what specific assumptions is the production possibilities curve based?

The assumption of the production possibilities curve is that there is a constant state of technology and resource use. Since resources are not perfectly shiftable, to obtain more of one will often require an increasing sacrifice.

EXERCISE 2 :

A. Describe the economic implications of Points A–F?

	INVESTMENTS	CONSUMER GOODS
Point A	60	0
Point B	Unattainable	
Point C	Unemployment	
Point D	40	55
Point E	25	60
Point F	0	65

B. What is the cost of moving from Point D to Point E?

To gain 5 more goods, one must give up 15 (40-25) investments.

C. Which allocations will lead to greater future growth?

Generally, investments lead to more capital goods and therefore more growth in the future. However, when an economy is in recession, more spending on goods can be beneficial.

EXERCISE **3** :

A. Revenue with 2 workers = 4 widgets @ $75 each = $300

    Cost with 2 workers = 2 @ $100 each   <u>$200</u>

                                         Profit = $100

B. Revenue with 3 workers = 5 widgets @ $60 each = $300

    Cost with 3 workers = 2 @ $100 each + 1 @ $60 =   <u>$260</u>

                                         Profit = $40

Another view of this process is that the additional or marginal benefit = $0 revenue and the marginal cost is $60. Therefore, it is not advisable to hire the additional worker as the marginal costs exceed marginal benefits.

MARKET
ALLOCATION OF SUPPLY AND DEMAND

INTRODUCTION

The allocation of resources within a capitalistic system is accomplished through a market approach. This is the seemingly simple idea that a buyer can trade money for goods or services provided by a seller. According to economic theory, then, the allocation of resources is accomplished through this basic demand and supply process. This theory assumes that no single buyer or any individual seller can actually have an impact on the market situation. The theory further assumes that demand behaviors and supply behaviors are shaped and positioned through the pricing system.

LEARNING OBJECTIVES

Please note the listed objectives. As you will see, the course materials are all objective driven.
This provides you with a constant way to direct and monitor your progress throughout the course.

1 OBJECTIVE ONE

Explain the overall role of demand and supply in the process of market allocation.

2 OBJECTIVE TWO

Describe in detail the nature of demand and the two essential types of change that occur with demand behavior.

3 OBJECTIVE THREE

Describe in detail the nature of supply and the two essential types of change that occur with supply behavior.

4 OBJECTIVE FOUR

Describe in detail how the interactions between demand and supply behaviors move a market toward equilibrium and how price functions as an allocation mechanism.

5 OBJECTIVE FIVE

Explain how government interventions in a market can create shortages and surpluses.

I INTERACTIVE EXERCISE

Use the major economic models to demonstrate an understanding of the chain-reactions resulting from human choices and how they move through an economy. Demonstrate an understanding of the tradeoffs that result.

Markets

Supply and demand are the two primary forces in market allocation. Supply is provided by producers and demand is created by consumers. The market is the interaction of these forces. A market system is most efficient if there is perfect (or pure) competition. Perfect competition is characterized by a very large number of both independent buyers and independent sellers. Two examples (although not "perfect" examples) are the stock market and an international bazaar.

In the 1920s Alfred Marshall addressed the relative importance of the supply side versus the demand side of the market. He compared supply and demand to the actions of a pair of scissors. Both blades of the scissors are equally important. The market is cleared (cut) by finding a price where producers are willing and able to supply (one blade) and consumers are willing and able to buy (the other blade).

Supply

Supply is created to satisfy consumer demand. Producers are continually seeking new opportunities to satisfy the needs of consumers. Supply is the response to the dollar votes of these consumers. Ultimately, then, it is the consumer who drives the allocation process. If a larger quantity of a particular item is demanded by consumers, then suppliers will increase their production of that item and will try to raise the price of that item.

A series of prices and individual quantities that producers are willing and able to produce at a particular point in time

Demand

Demand is determined by the sovereign (independent) consumer. When a consumer purchases a product, a demand is created for this item to be restocked by the merchant. This idea is the origin of the saying, "the dollar votes when an item is purchased." Ultimately, consumer sovereignty determines what is produced in a market-based economy.

A series of prices and individual quantities that consumers are willing and able to buy at a particular point in time

Demand, then, is the relationship between the possible prices of a product and the quantities of that product that would be demanded by the consumers. Stated a bit differently, demand is the series of prices and the related quantities that consumers are willing and able to buy at a particular point in time.

LAW OF DEMAND

The law of demand assumes there is an inverse relationship between price and the quantity demanded. The amount of a product which consumers are willing and able to purchase at a particular price is called the quantity demanded. When price increases, the **quantity demanded** by consumers <u>decreases</u>. When price decreases the quantity demanded by consumers increases if all other influences remain the same. A consumer might purchase only three units of a product at $8, but actually buy five units of the product at $6. Thus, as price decreases the **quantity demanded** increases.

The *total* market demand for goods or services consists of the sum of the individual demand relationships of all possible buyers. Some individuals will be willing and able to pay more for a particular good. Some individuals will be willing and able to buy more units at a certain price. The total market demand, then, may be found by summing all of the individual demand behaviors.

Inverse Demand Relationship

There are three reasons why price and quantity demanded have an *inverse* relationship (move in opposite directions). The first reason is the **income effect**. If price decreases, a consumer is willing to buy more at the lower price. At lower prices the consumer has more purchasing power and this is called the income effect.

The second reason for the inverse relationship is called the **substitution effect**. If the price of item A, a substitute for item B, decreases, then people will buy more of A and less of B. Thus the quantity demanded of A will increase when its price decreases.

The third reason for the inverse relationship is called the **law of diminishing marginal utility**. Economists assume that at any given price a person will continue to consume more and more of an item, but at some point that person starts receiving less and less additional satisfaction (utility) from each additional unit consumed. Therefore, beyond some point, the consumer will only purchase more of that item if the price of that item decreases.

In summary, the reasons given above for "inverse demand relationships" provide us the somewhat more technical analysis for human behavior that we all instinctively understand—when the price of something goes down, we (as a group) buy more of it. But there is much more to our study of demand and supply than "price down, we buy more."

There are three basic methods of analysis that we will use in our study of demand and supply. We will use descriptive analysis, tabular analysis and graphical analysis. We have already used "descriptive analysis" (word-/concept-based analysis) in presenting the discussion above. We can now expand on these concepts using the tabular and the graphical approach.

Consider the tabulation of prices and quantities demanded in the illustration below:

Price	Quantity Demanded
$10	1
9	2
8	3
7	4
6	5

This table of prices and quantities is called a demand schedule.

Demand Schedule and the Graph

This schedule is describing the change in quantity demanded as price decreases from $10 to $6. The entire set of prices and quantities is referred to as "demand." The demand for a product, then, describes the quantities of goods and services that consumers are willing and able to purchase as a function of prices at a given point in time.

Graphically, a demand line is always plotted with price on the y-axis and quantity on the x-axis. The negative slope (downward trend) of a demand line illustrates the "inverse relationship" described earlier—as prices increase, quantity demanded decreases and as price decreases, quantity demanded increases. The data from the demand schedule above is plotted on the demand graph. A change in quantity demanded is shown by a movement along the demand line. As one example, notice that when the price decreases from $9 to $7, the quantity demanded will increase from two units to four units.

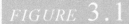

FIGURE 3.1

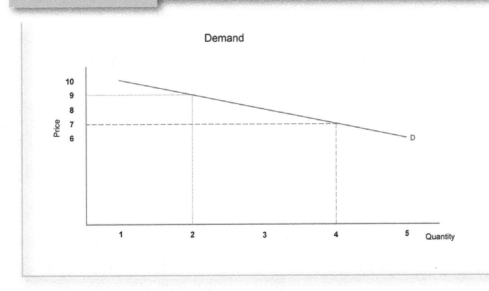

A change in price is, in fact, the only reason why there can be a "change in quantity demanded." If a factor other than price changes (such as income), then we will see a "change in demand" (notice the word "quantity" is <u>not</u> included in that last phrase).

In the next section we will explore this idea of "change in demand." A quick preview: For several reasons a consumer may view a product differently as time moves along. A consumer may either decide to buy more at a given price—or buy less at that same price. In either instance, the quantity demanded at that price has changed. Example—In the illustration above we observed a consumer buying two units of product when the price was $9. What might cause that same consumer to buy four units of the product even though the price stays exactly the same at $9? In the next section we will begin to answer that question.

Changes in Demand

A demand line may shift right, representing an increase in a demand behavior . . . or shift left, representing a decrease in that demand behavior. Circumstances affecting demand can change for many reasons. For example, consider the change in demand for a seasonal item such as sun screen lotion. A change in demand for the item is represented by adding a second demand schedule. If conditions favor sale of the item (summer time), then the second schedule (D2) lies to the right of the original schedule (D1). If the change in demand is constant, then the slope of the new D2 behavior will be the same as the slope of the original D1 behavior. Notice below that for every price, the increased demand schedule D2 shows two more units demanded than the original (winter time) demand schedule D1.

Price	Quantity Demanded 1	Quantity Demanded 2
$10	1	3
9	2	4
8	3	5
7	4	6
6	5	7

Because the quantities demanded increase at each price level, an "increase in demand" will always cause a right shift of the demand line (see Figure 3.2). If the quantities demanded decrease at each price level, the "decrease in demand" will always cause a left shift of the demand line.

FIGURE 3.2

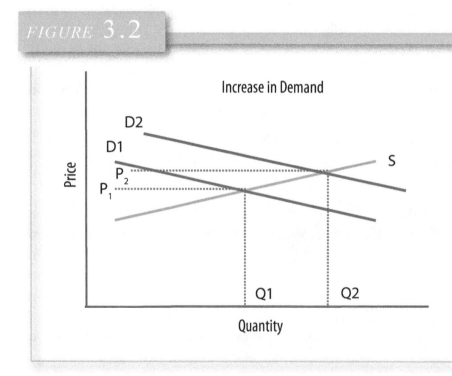

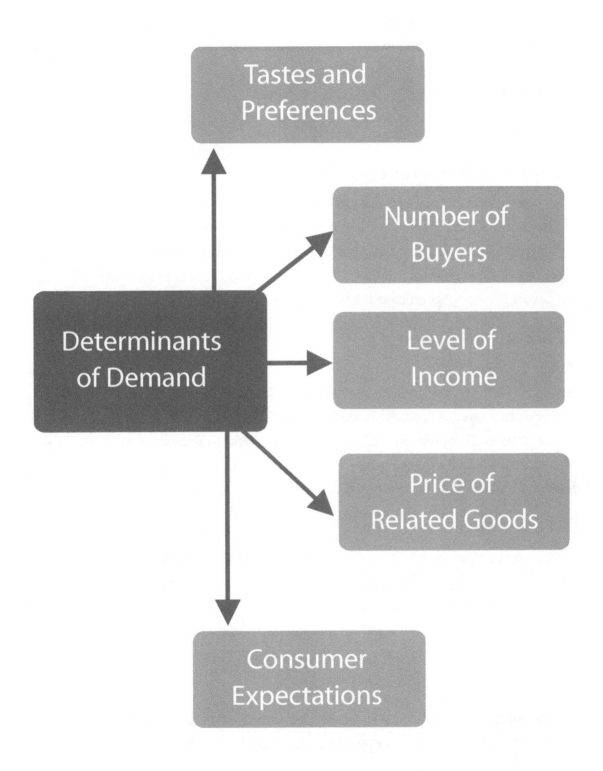

Determinants of Demand

When we describe the **determinants of demand** we are saying that a change in any one of these fundamental factors will cause a consumer to buy more or less of a product at each price level. In effect, a change in any one of these fundamental factors will cause a demand line to *shift*.

The **five** primary determinants of demand are:

Tastes and Preferences:

When consumers decide that one particular cell phone is much more desirable than another, the demand for this particular cell phone will increase (the demand line will shift right). The demand for the other cell phone brands will, *other factors remaining the same*, diminish (shift left). Given a moment's thought, it is evident that advertising can have a great impact on consumers' tastes and preferences.

Number of Buyers:

If there are simply more people available to purchase a product at every price level, an increase in demand (shift right) will result. If fewer people are available to purchase at every price level, a decrease in demand (shift left) will result. This can occur when there is an overall population change, a geographic shift in population or a demographic change. For example, if more babies are being born in a certain part of the country, the demand for diapers (more new parents) will increase at every price level (right shift).

Level of Income:

If people have more income, they will purchase *more* of items known as normal goods. Normal goods (sometimes called "superior goods") are items that consumers will instinctively increase their purchases of when they have an increase in income. An example of a normal good is a new automobile. An increase in the incomes of families across the country will typically result in an increase in the quantity of *new* cars being demanded (as opposed to "used cars").

An **inferior good** is one that consumers will buy *less* of when their incomes increase (other factors remaining the same). An example of an "inferior good" would, then, be the *used* car.

Price of Related Goods:

Two products that are viewed as replacements for each other are called **substitute** goods. Two goods that are purchased and consumed together are called **complementary** goods.

When two goods are *substitutes*, a change in the price of one will cause a change in the demand of the other in the <u>same</u> direction. When two goods are *complementary* goods, a change in the price of one will cause a change in the demand of the other in the *opposite* direction.

An example of a substitute situation is the relationship between Coke and Pepsi in the soft drink market. If the price of Pepsi *decreases* dramatically (think "half-price sale"), then the demand for Coke would *decrease* (shift to the left). An increase in the price of a substitute will cause an increase in the demand for the other item.

An example of two goods that are complementary would be computers and computer software. Each is directly related to the other and they are often purchased together. When the price of computers *decreases*, then more software will be purchased (an *increase* in software demand). If the price of computers increased dramatically for some reason, then less software would be purchased (a *decrease* in software demand).

Consumer Expectations:

If consumers expect the price of an item to *increase* in the future, they will tend to increase their *present* demand for the item. On the other hand, if consumers think that the price of the item will go down in the future, they will tend to decrease their present demand for that item. The demand for houses during the past 10 years has been an interesting example of changes in consumer expectations.

In our discussions up to this point, we have not yet seen any examples of exactly how the market price of an item is actually established. We must involve supply in our discussion to create these examples. At this point, the examples of demand display a *series of prices* and the *quantities demanded* that correspond to those prices. We have displayed demand both in tabular form as well as graphically. Now it is time to bring supply into the analysis.

SUPPLY

Conceptually, supply and demand are closely related in that both describe human behavior in relation to the price of a product. With supply, however, we are describing the amount of a product that *business people* are willing and able to create at a moment in time (as opposed to the buying behavior of consumers). For "supply behavior" the relationship between price and quantity is direct, rather than inverse as it is with "demand behavior." For supply, then, a higher price will result in a higher quantity produced (a "direct" relationship). A lower price will result in a lower quantity produced (again, a "direct" relationship). Graphically we can say that the supply curve will slope upward and to the right.

The Law of Supply

The law of supply is based on the "direct relationship" noted above. The law of supply summarizes the direct relationship between price and the quantity supplied by producers. If price increases, then the *quantity* supplied will also increase. The law of supply simply states that this direct relationship exists between price and quantity supplied at *every* level. When prices go up, greater quantities will be provided by producers at these higher price levels, all other factors remaining the same (remember our "ceteris paribus" from Lesson One).

The supply curve for the total market is simply the summation of all suppliers' reactions to the various possible changes in price. Even though each *individual* producer tends to have a different reaction to a price change, the total quantity brought to the market by all producers at each new price is what creates the supply curve (or supply line).

Since an increase in price leads to an increase in *quantity* supplied, the supply line slopes upward and to the right. As with the demand line, price is on the y-axis and quantity is on the x-axis.

FIGURE 3.3

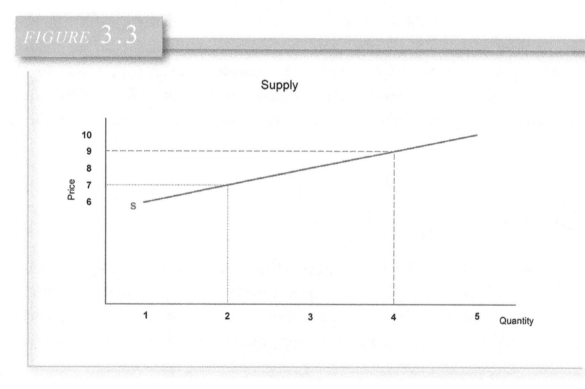

A **change in quantity supplied** is a movement along a given supply line. This is caused by a change in price. An increase in price is the only variable that will increase the amount brought to the market by producers if all other variables remain the same.

Price	Quantity Supplied
$10	5
9	4
8	3
7	2

A **change in supply** is a shift in the entire supply line as more or fewer units of product are brought to the market by producers at a given price.

FIGURE 3.4

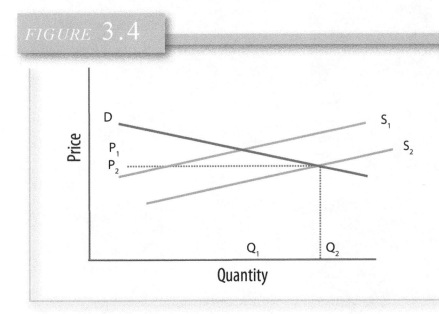

If there is an overall increase in suppliers' costs of production (e.g., wage costs go up), there will be fewer units of product brought to the market at each price level . . . a *left shift* in the supply line.

If, however, there is an overall decrease in suppliers' costs of production (e.g., wage costs go down), there will be more units of product brought to the market at each price level, a right shift in the supply line.

Determinants of Supply

- Resource Costs
- Number of Producers
- Production Substitute
- Future Prices
- Taxes or Subsidies
- Technology

Price	Quantity Supplied 1	Quantity Supplied 2
$10	5	10
9	4	9
8	3	8
7	2	7

An illustration of an increase in the supply is shown in Figure 3.4 with a change from S_1 to S_2.

Determinants of Supply

Just as with "change in demand," the phrase "change in supply" means that something other than price has changed. Remember that when price changes only quantity supplied will change as we move along the supply line. But when there is a "change in supply", the entire supply line will shift. We must re-plot the tabular data when the supply line shifts—either left (a decrease in supply) . . . or right (an increase in supply).

When we describe the **determinants of supply** we are saying that a change in any one of these fundamental factors will cause producers to create more or less of a product at each price level. In effect, a change in any one of these fundamental factors will cause a supply line to shift.

The **six** primary determinants of supply are:

Resource Costs:

Any increase in resource costs (that is, "factor of production" costs) will shift the supply line to the left. Any decrease in those costs will shift the supply line to the right. Examples—An *increase in the cost* of oil (or labor) will cause the supply line to decrease (shift left). A *decrease in the cost* of labor (or capital equipment) will cause the supply line to increase (shift right).

Number of Producers:

Any change in the number of businesses in a particular industry will also shift the supply line. Example—Fewer suppliers of airline transportation services will cause the supply line of "seats available" to decrease (shift left). More suppliers of ocean cruise line entertainment services will cause the supply line of "cabins available" to increase (shift right).

Price of a Production Substitute:

An item that suppliers can produce in place of their current product is called a "production substitute." A change in the market price of a "production substitute" can cause an increase or decrease in the overall supply of the current product being produced. If many farmers are currently growing wheat but the market price of corn increases dramatically, then with the next planting those farmers may substitute corn for wheat production. This would result in a decrease in the supply of wheat (a left shift).

Conversely, if the market price of corn dramatically decreases, then with the next planting even more farmers will be producing wheat. This will result in an increase in the supply of wheat (a right shift).

Expectations about Future Prices:

Expected improvements in resource costs that may cause producers to shift the supply line to the left. Expected decreases in those costs may cause the supply line to shift to the right. Examples—Addition of a new tax may cause the supply line to decrease (shift left). An improvement of capital equipment may cause the supply line to increase (shift right). Such changes may occur dependent upon producer expectations of future competition.

Taxes or Subsidies:

If increased taxes are imposed on producers in a particular industry, fewer units of that item will be supplied at each price level (a left shift). However, if government provides subsidies (money to increase production), then suppliers will provide more of that item at every price level (a right shift).

Technology:

If there is an improvement in the technology used to produce an item, this will cause an increase in supply (a right shift). Improvements in technology such as robotic manufacturing and other forms of automation can reduce production costs which, in turn, will drive the increase in supply (the right shift).

Market equilibrium

As consumers, we want the lowest price—as producers in the Circular Flow we want the highest price. The market price or "**equilibrium**" price is where we try to get together. The equilibrium price is established where consumers as a group are willing and able to buy exactly that quantity that producers (as a group) are willing and able to produce. At the **equilibrium price** every unit produced will be purchased—there will be no surplus left over and there will be no shortage of the product.

We need to keep in mind that markets provide that very valuable "allocation" function in our economy. Markets allocate resources and they do this primarily through the rationing effect of prices. A product's price reflects its relative scarcity. If a product becomes relatively more scarce (as would occur with an increase in demand or a decrease in supply) we would expect the market price to increase to reflect this increased scarcity. If the opposite occurs—a decrease in demand or an increase in supply—the product's equilibrium price will drop (the product is "less scarce").

Assumptions:

Free market allocation of products and services is determined by the interaction of the demand created by consumers and the supply created by producers. Price determines the quantity demanded by the consumers and the quantity supplied by the producers. Recall that the law of demand states that there is an <u>inverse</u> relationship between price and quantity demanded while the law of supply states that there is a direct relationship between price and quantity supplied.

The laws of supply and demand work together creating market **equilibrium**. The end result of this dynamic process is a market clearing price where the quantity demanded by consumers *becomes exactly equal* to the quantity supplied by producers. Ongoing adjustments in both buying behavior and production behavior allocate resources *toward* this market equilibrium. Note in Figure 3.5 of market equilibrium that a market equilibrium exists when quantity demanded = quantity supplied at 3 units and a price of $8. The **forces of adjustment** *toward* market equilibrium are the natural instincts of suppliers toward making profit and the natural instincts of consumers toward satisfying their wants (gaining utility).

If the current price of a good is below the equilibrium price, then quantity demanded by consumers will be *more* than the quantity supplied by producers. This will result in a **shortage**. A shortage will exist whenever the quantity demanded is more than the quantity supplied. In this situation the producers will increase their asking price *and* their quantity supplied. Producers will continue with this approach until they realize that they are producing too much and have raised the price too high.

FIGURE 3.5

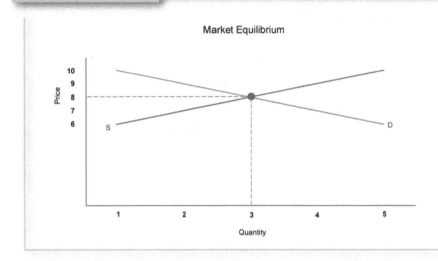

Market Equilibrium

If the current price of a good is above the equilibrium price, then quantity demanded by consumers will be *less* than the quantity supplied by producers. This will result in a **surplus**. A surplus will exist whenever the quantity demanded is less than the quantity supplied. In this situation the producers will decrease their asking price *and* their quantity supplied. Producers will continue with this approach until they realize that they are producing too little and have lowered the price too much.

If the current price of a good becomes exactly equal to the equilibrium price, then quantity demanded by consumers will be the *same* as the quantity supplied by producers. An equilibrium is established at that price where producers are willing to supply exactly the same amount of product as consumers are willing to purchase. In this situation (which usually does *not* last very long) the producers will have no incentive to change either their asking price *or* their quantity supplied. Producers will stay with their present approach until they realize that there has been (or will be) a *shift* in demand or in supply within their industry. These shifts are usually not far away in the "real world" and, in fact, often occur before an equilibrium is ever actually achieved . . . that is, *before* the asking price for a product rises or falls enough to become equal to the equilibrium price.

Shifts in demand or supply cause changes in market equilibrium and changes in the *location* of the *equilibrium price* and the *equilibrium quantity*. As expected an increase in demand (shift right) with supply remaining constant will create an increase in the equilibrium price and an increase in the equilibrium quantity. Also, as expected, a decrease in supply (shift left) with demand remaining constant will yield an increase in the equilibrium price and a decrease in the equilibrium quantity. The resulting shortages *or* surpluses drive the markets toward these new equilibrium points. Once again, in the "real world" another shift in behavior often arrives before a market can really settle into its current equilibrium.

Complex shifts occur when *both* supply behavior and demand behavior shift at the same time. Both equilibrium price and equilibrium quantity will change, but the direction of these changes (increase or decrease) will be *indeterminate* until the magnitudes of the changes are considered. To illustrate such a "complex shift," one must draw two sketches of the shifts in the behavior lines. For example, the first sketch of a complex right shift would consider a *small* increase in demand along with a *moderate* increase in supply. The second sketch would consider a *large* increase in demand along with that *same* moderate increase in supply.

If both demand and supply decrease (shift left), the outcome on price is **indeterminate** (until the magnitudes of the demand shift is considered), but the equilibrium quantity definitely declines. If both demand and supply increase (shift right), the outcome on price is indeterminate, but equilibrium quantity definitely rises. If demand shifts right and supply shifts left, equilibrium price will definitely rise, but equilibrium quantity is indeterminate until the magnitudes of the shifts are considered.

For **complex shifts** it is very important to sketch the magnitudes of the shifts as well as the direction of the shifts that are being considered.

At this point it is also very important to recall and reflect upon the idea that in a market system prices function as a **rationing mechanism**. It is the market price that places a limit on the amount of a product that a consumer is willing and able to purchase. And it is the market price that places a limit on the amount of resources that a business person is willing and able to commit in the creation of that product.

A market-clearing price ensures that those willing and able to pay that clearing price will receive the product, but those unwilling (or unable) to pay that price will *not* receive the product. Depending upon the product and the circumstances, this can seem a very harsh reality. It is for this reason that most societies have some blend of tradition-based *and* government-based approaches to complement the market-based approach.

We should also keep in mind that over the long run only those suppliers who are willing to *accept* a market-clearing price from consumers will, in fact, be able sell their product. *Over the long run,* those suppliers who are seeking a higher price and are unwilling to accept a market-clearing price will usually not survive.

GOVERNMENT INTERVENTION

FIGURE 3.6

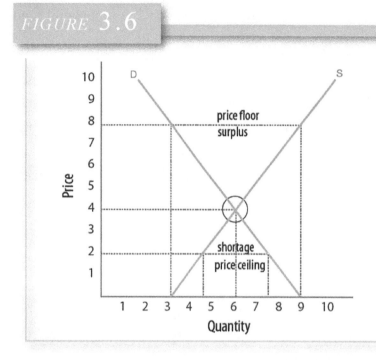

It was previously mentioned that most societies include some government-based actions to complement a system that is essentially market-based. Direct government intervention into the pricing of a product is one such action. This particular type of action can be very controversial. A direct government intervention into pricing will change both the quantity of product supplied and the quantity of the product demanded. Notice in the graph in Figure 3.6 that equilibrium *without* government intervention is at price of $4 and a quantity of 6 units. But if a **price ceiling** at $2 is imposed, then the quantity supplied is 4.5 units and the quantity demanded is 7.5 units. This results in a shortage of 3 units. If a **price floor** is imposed at $8, then the resulting quantity demanded is 3 units and the quantity supplied is 9 units. This results in a surplus of 6 units.

Price Ceiling

A price ceiling is created when a government sets a legal *maximum* price on a product in order to keep the product price below the true equilibrium price. The term "price ceiling" is used because by law it places a "cap" on the price that can be charged for the product. The "price ceiling," however, will result in the quantity demanded by consumers being greater than the quantity supplied by producers. This means there will be a shortage of that product. An example of a "price ceiling" is when government sets a maximum rent that can be charged for an apartment. This results in more rentals being desired by consumers . . . but fewer rentals being supplied by developers (a shortage of apartments).

Price Floor

A price floor is created when a government sets a legal *minimum* price on a product in order to keep the product price above the true equilibrium price. The term "price floor" is used because by law it creates a "support" for the price that can be charged for the product or service. The "price floor," however, will result in the quantity demanded by the buyers being less than the quantity supplied by the sellers. This means there will be a surplus of the item in the market place. An example of a "price floor" is minimum wage legislation. Firms are required by law to pay the minimum wage even though the equilibrium wage in that particular labor market may be somewhat lower. The minimum wage (price floor) increases the quantity of labor supplied by households in the Circular Flow, but reduces the quantity of labor demanded by businesses. Yes, this tends to result in a surplus of labor, also know as "unemployment." This is a topic we will certainly be spending more time with in the lessons that follow.

Introduction to Microeconomics

Macroeconomic growth is a bridge to microeconomics. The concepts developed in Unit One are the basic tools shared by both macroeconomics and microeconomics. In Lesson One the basic terminology of economics was studied. Basic models of production possibilities and circular flow were presented in Lesson Two. And, in Lesson Three we studied supply and demand for individual products/services. In concluding this unit we will begin our discussion of microeconomics using the basic tools from economics applied in macro markets for growth and then bridge to traditional microeconomic topics.

The Macroeconomic Environment within Microeconomics

Microeconomics concerns allocation systems by firms and consumers. However, the macroeconomic environment influences both firms and consumers. Both must adjust to some variables outside of their own control called exogenous variables. In Lesson Five we consider the macroeconomic exogenous variables as an introduction to Unit Two and then consider other variables that are within the control of firms and individuals, called endogenous variables.

Exogenous Variables of Microeconomic Allocation

There are many exogenous variables impacting microeconomic systems. Firms and individuals must consider exogenous factors such as the condition of the economy as a whole, the international and national political environment, resource prices as well as global sustainability issues. The single most important factor for firms and consumers is the condition of the national economy. Macroeconomic conditions and growth set significant parameters for microeconomic units.

The Impact of Economic Growth on Consumers and Firms

Economic growth is defined as an increase in real gross domestic product (GDP) or increases in real GDP per capita. The latter figure compares the growth of goods and services with growth in population. If GDP real growth is not greater than population growth, then consumption per person declines.

Firms and consumers are sensitive to national economic growth. Consider how different an environment is when consumers are without work. During a recession, individuals lose their purchasing power and firms lose customers. Most firms and consumers experience economic cyclical variation, having more resources with national economic growth and less with recession.

The Primary Factors of Macroeconomic Growth

- The amount of resources used
- Technology
- Education and training of workers
- The number of workers
- Opportunity cost of resource inputs
- Amount and quality of capital utilized
- Availability of savings for investment

Economic growth occurs from either using more resources or better using the existing resources. Productivity is better use of resources. Productivity is generally measured as an increase in output per worker-hour. Most economic growth is due to productivity gains caused by better use of capital, technology, and training. However, economic growth by increased productivity alone is difficult for a nation without attendant increases in the number of workers and the natural resource base.

American Growth

For economists, economic growth is an ongoing study. In the 1950's the growth model of Solow-Swan emphasized the importance of capital and investment. In the 1980s through 1990s the Lucas-Barro model emphasized the importance of technology through human capital (knowledge, education, and skills).

The United States has experienced much growth over the last 200 years with significant increases in the standard of living. American real (inflation adjusted) GDP growth has averaged about 3.5 percent per year and 3.2 percent per year in real GDP per capita over the last 50 years. Although the growth has been cyclical, over most decades there has been growth. However, the rate of growth has slowed recently.

Current Economic Growth Implications

For both firms and individuals the allocation of resources is partly determined by the national economic conditions. In order to adapt to macroeconomic conditions, a firm must control costs and consider total revenue factors while an individual must control expenditures and seek higher income by adapting skills to labor demand.

Endogenous Variables for the Consumer, "King of Capitalist Allocation"

One of the most important endogenous elements for consumers and firms is product price. Economists have analyzed the behavior of consumers to changes in prices for many years. Consumers have a threshold price for purchasing or not purchasing a good or service. Each of us has memorized prices for some items and we make our purchasing decision based on what is a "good buy." Firms must understand consumer behavior and the role of price in allocation.

Elasticity of Demand

Sensitivity of consumers to prices is our first topic of microeconomics following in Lesson Five.

Demand is a schedule showing a series of prices and quantities that consumers would be willing and able to buy at a specific point in time.

Determinants of Demand are changes in tastes, income, number of buyers, consumer expectations and prices of related goods that cause a fundamental change in the way consumers view a particular product or service.

Determinants of Supply are changes in resource prices, technology, expectations, related goods pricing, taxes and subsidies, and the number of producers that cause a fundamental change in the way producers view a particular product or service.

Equilibrium is that point in an individual market where quantity demanded equals quantity supplied. It is always where the supply and demand curves cross—the market is cleared with no surplus or shortage.

Law of Demand assumes an inverse relationship between price and quantity. At a higher price, quantity demanded declines—at a lower price, quantity demanded increases.

Law of Supply assumes a direct relationship between price and quantity. At a higher price, producers will produce more. At a lower price, the quantity supplied will decline.

Market Shortage occurs when the quantity demanded is greater than the quantity supplied.

Market Surplus occurs when the quantity supplied is greater than the quantity demanded.

Market System is where buyers and sellers meet. It provides for the free interaction of buyer and seller in the marketplace.

Price Ceiling is a situation when government sets a price that is below the equilibrium price.

Price Floor is a situation when government sets a price that is above the equilibrium price.

Price Function in a market, price measures scarcity. If the product is more scarce, price goes up; if less scarce, price will go down. Price is an important mechanism for allocating scarce resources in a market.

Pure Competition occurs when a large number of independently acting buyers and sellers are present in a market place where no one producer can unduly affect that market.

Quantity Demanded On a demand schedule, this is the amount that corresponds to one price. A change in price will change the quantity demanded.

Quantity Supplied On a supply schedule, this is the amount that corresponds to one price. A change in price will change the quantity supplied.

APPLIED EXERCISES

EXERCISE 1:

Given the following demand and supply for cell phones, respond to the questions below.

Quantity Demanded	Price	Quantity Supplied
100	$300	500
200	200	400
300	100	300
400	50	200

A: What are the equilibrium price and quantity in this market?

B: What occurs at a price of $300?

C: What occurs at a price of $50?

D: What would happen if government sets a price ceiling at $50?

EXERCISE 2:

What effect would each of the following have on the **demand** for cell phones?

A: The price of cell phones increases due to an increase in a component part?

B: There is an increase in income for most families.

C: Consumers anticipate the price of cell phones will be lower in the future.

D: There is a decrease in incomes caused by recession.

E: There is an increase in telephone connect charges required for cell phones.

APPLIED EXERCISES

EXERCISE 3 :

What effect would each of the following have on the **supply** for cell phones?

A: The government increases taxes on cell phone usage.

B: A decline in the number of cell phone firms in the industry.

C: The expectation that cell phones will be cheaper in the future.

D: Technology improves the processes for making cell phones.

E: The government provides a subsidy to cell phone production.

EXERCISE 4 :

What effect will each of the changes in supply and demand have on **equilibrium price** and **quantity**?

A: Demand increases and supply is constant.

B: Supply decreases and demand is constant.

C: Demand decreases and supply is constant.

D: Demand increases and supply increases.

E: Supply decreases and demand increases.

APPLIED EXERCISES: ANSWERS

EXERCISE 1:

A. What are the equilibrium price and quantity in this market?

Quantity = 300 @ Price = $100

B. What occurs at a price of $300?

Quantity Supplied = 500; Quantity Demanded = 100; Surplus = 400

C. What occurs at a price of $50?

Quantity Demanded = 400; Quantity Supplied = 200; Shortage 200

D. What would happen if government sets a price ceiling at $50?

Quantity Demanded = 400; Quantity Supplied = 200; Shortage of 200

EXERCISE 2:

A. The price of cell phones increases due to an increase in a component part?

No change to demand, only a movement along a demand line (change in quantity demanded).

B. There is an increase in income for most families.

Increase in demand because a cell phone is a superior or normal good, more will be purchased at every price with an increase in income.

C. Consumers anticipate the price of cell phones will be lower in the future.

Decrease in demand as consumers wait to make purchases.

D. There is a decrease in incomes caused by recession.

Decrease in demand because a cell phone is a superior or normal good.

E. There is an increase in telephone connect charges required for cell phones.

Decrease in demand because of an increase in the price of a complement (cell phones and cell phone service).

APPLIED EXERCISES: ANSWERS

EXERCISE 3:

A. The government increases taxes on cell phone usage.
   Decrease in supply.

B. A decline in the number of cell phone firms in the industry.
   Decrease in supply.

C. The expectation that cell phones will be cheaper in the future.
   Increase in supply.

D. Technology improves the processes for making cell phones.
   Decrease in costs leads to increases in supply.

E. The government provides a subsidy to cell phone production.
   Increase in supply.

EXERCISE 4:

A. Demand increases and supply is constant.
   Increase in equilibrium price and quantity.

B. Supply decreases and demand is constant.
   Decrease in equilibrium quantity and increase in price.

C. Demand decreases and supply is constant.
   Decrease in equilibrium price and quantity.

D. Demand increases and supply increases.
   Increase in equilibrium quantity and indeterminate change in price.

E. Supply decreases and demand increases.
   Increase in equilibrium price and indeterminate change in quantity.

INTRODUCTION

Lesson 4 will analyze supply and demand allocation with efficient and inefficient market outcomes. In addition, we will consider how government can impact markets in an attempt to improve efficiency.

LEARNING OBJECTIVES

Please note the listed objectives. As you will see, the course materials are all objective driven. This provides you with a constant way to direct and monitor your progress throughout the course.

1 OBJECTIVE ONE

Describe an Efficient Market, the Benefits, and how an Efficient Market is maintained.

2 OBJECTIVE TWO

Explain a Market Failure and describe the causes and consequences.

3 OBJECTIVE THREE

List the types of Market Failures.

4 OBJECTIVE FOUR

Describe and illustrate Positive and Negative Externalities.

5 OBJECTIVE FIVE

Describe how government can impact a Market Failure.

I INTERACTIVE EXERCISE

Explain the debate of government involvement in Market Failures.

Our discussion features market systems related to the following topics:

- Economic Efficiency as a Goal of Economics (Benefits of Efficiency)
- The Early Economic History of Efficiency: Pareto Optimality
- The Necessary Process for Efficiency
- Socially Optimal Efficiency: MB = MC
- Theory of Inefficient Markets (Market Failures)
- Causes of Market Failure
- Consequences of Market Failure: Deadweight Loss
  - Over Production
  - Under Production
- Factors Influencing Market Failure
  - Consumer Surplus
  - Producer Surplus
- Examples of Market Failures
  - Market Externalities
  - Monopoly Power
  - Public Goods Inefficiency: Nonmarket Allocation, Free Rider, and Moral Hazard
- The Debate of Government Efficiency and Intervention in Inefficient Markets

REVIEW OF EFFICIENT MARKETS

Lesson 2 describes the benefits of an efficient market that will "produce the maximum output of desirable items with a given input." Productively efficient is discussed in Lesson 2 as a market providing maximum output with a minimum resource input. Economically efficiency in allocation is described as productively efficient but also supplying maximum consumer needs.

Lesson 3 discusses how efficient resource allocation is attained and maintained through the free market forces using mechanisms of supply and demand. A competitive, efficient market occurs when market mechanisms result in maximum satisfaction. With equilibrium of supply and demand, market clearing exists with no resulting surplus or shortage. Economists assume that consumer satisfaction (consumer surplus) and supplier satisfaction (producer surplus) are maximized when resources are efficiently allocated.

BEHAVIOR OF INEFFICIENT MARKET

Competitive markets are assumed to be efficient, but an inefficient, market failure involves a disequilibrium in allocation. This disequilibrium is present because consumers do not pay full price and/or suppliers do not pay the full cost of production. A market failure results in an over allocation or under allocation of goods with a loss of potential output and loss of potential satisfaction.

The Economic History of Efficiency Conditions: Pareto Optimality

According to the Neoclassical Theory of Economics in the early 1900s and evolving into Welfare Economics in the 1920s, the greater the satisfaction an individual adds to the economy, the greater the prosperity for this individual and society. An efficient individual's interplay with market forces creates value added for a maximum output for society and maximum individual benefit without disadvantage to other individuals' welfare.

TABLE 4.1

	PRODUCTION POSSIBILITIES CURVE OF COMPUTER AND CLOTHING OUTPUT	
Point	Units of Computers	Units of Clothing
A	9	2
B	6	6
C	2	9
D	3	4

Welfare theory within microeconomics assumes maximum individual well-being is the goal of resource allocation. Welfare Theory free market efficiency was illustrated by Pareto Optimality and this became a measure of microeconomic vitality. The concept of Pareto Optimality was published by Vilfredo Pareto, an Italian economist, in the early 1920s. According to Pareto's theory, an efficient, optimal system exists when no change in allocation among participants can be made that would yield an increased benefit (satisfaction) to one individual without making another individual worse off. In optimality, maximum satisfaction is individually achieved within a competitive market and results in maximum satisfaction for the macro economy.

The production possibilities model and production frontier (PPF) from Lesson 2 can be used to illustrate a movement toward Pareto Optimality. In Figure 4.1 output at point B is an improvement toward Pareto Optimality relative to point D. At point B more clothing and more computers are produced compared to point D. This is an improvement in Pareto Efficiency because more benefit is produced for all individuals in the society without a loss to any one individual (this assumes the same relative distribution of the products as occurred at Point D). Points A and C are not movements toward Pareto Efficiency because less clothing is produced at A than at D and fewer computers are produced at point C than at point D. Individuals who prefer clothing would be worse off with a movement from D to A. Individuals who prefer computers would be worse off with a movement from D to C. An improvement in Pareto Efficiency exists only if no individual's welfare is sacrificed.

FIGURE 4.1

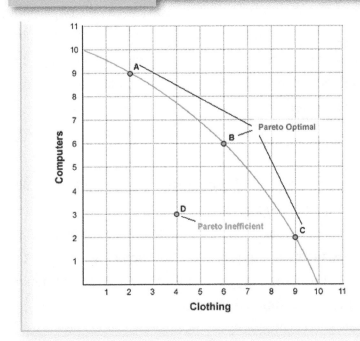

GRAPH OF PRODUCTION POSSIBILITIES CURVE FROM TABLE 4.1

Conditions and Dynamics of an Efficient Market

In 1776 Adam Smith, the "Father of Economics," described an efficient, competitive market system as the result of the "invisible hand of allocation." An efficient, modern economy also assumes that there is an invisible hand through "maximum competition" when:

- many buyers and many sellers freely participate in the market,
- no one consumer or producer is able to influence the price,
- any producer can enter or leave the market,
- prices/costs are fully incurred by consumers and producers respectively,
- and allocations are rationed by price through the mechanisms of supply and demand.

Given these conditions, there is a dynamic adjustment toward equilibrium with efficiency. If quantity supplied is temporarily greater than quantity demanded, there is an oversupply (over production) and prices will drop until equilibrium is restored where quantity supplied equals quantity demanded. If quantity demanded is temporarily greater than quantity supplied, there is an under supply (under production) and prices will increase until equilibrium is restored where quantity supplied equals quantity demanded.

Price Rationing Assumptions of Competitive Allocation

A free market demand line is comprised of consumers willing to pay a <u>full price</u> and the supply line includes <u>all societal costs</u> of producing the good. Full price means that all factors of land, labor, capital, and entrepreneurship related to price are paid by the consumer and full cost means that all factors of land, labor, capital, and entrepreneurship related to production are paid by the supplier.

Price versus Value

In a market with output at any point other than equilibrium of supply and demand, some consumers and/or some producers value the good at more or less than the market price. The phrase "getting your money's worth" is the concept of <u>value</u>. The price and value of an item are differentiated within economics. <u>Value</u> is what consumers are willing to pay for additional satisfaction (marginal benefit) and <u>price</u> is the charge for the additional benefit (market price is what is paid for the additional benefit).

The concept of value is quantified within the market as the opportunity cost. Consumer value is what consumers are willing to give up of other goods to receive a product. For a producer, value is what suppliers are willing to supply of a good and not produce something else with the same resources. On the other hand, price for consumers and producers is what is paid and is determined through the market. In an efficient market the value is the same as the market price and costs.

Consumer Value versus Price

To illustrate an efficient market, consider that you decide to buy a lunch at a fast-food market shown in Table 4.2. The lunch is set at a market price of $8.50. Your purchase means that you are willing to give up $8.50 of other products to get this lunch's marginal benefit; the value you place on the lunch is the value added. If the lunch is fully price allocated (price includes all consumer cost factors of the meal) at $8.50 and you give up spending the $8.50 for other goods, then the price is the same as the value of foregone goods. At this price the value and market price are equal for you. The additional benefit, additional satisfaction, assumed for eating the meal, is the value added or <u>marginal benefit</u>. Marginal benefit as value is the reason consumers purchase an additional good in microeconomic theory.

TABLE 4.2

EXAMPLE OF SUPPLY AND DEMAND FOR A LUNCH AT A FAST-FOOD RESTAURANT

Quantity Demanded	Price	Quantity Supplied
0	$ 10.00	6
1	9.50	5
2	9.00	4
3	8.50	3
4	8.00	2
5	7.50	1
6	7.00	0

Producer Value versus Price

The $8.50 priced lunch was also value priced by the supplier at this point because the producer was willing to make this lunch and not make other goods with these resources. For suppliers the <u>marginal cost</u> of the lunch is the additional cost to produce one more lunch. Marginal cost as value is the major criteria suppliers use to determine whether or not to produce an additional good in microeconomic theory.

Consumer Value = Price = Producer Value: Market Equilibrium of Maximum Output

Consumers are willing to give up buying $8.50 of other goods and producers are willing to supply the product and forgo supplying other goods at this full value/market price. If the price and costs are fully incurred with no subsidies or grants given to consumers or suppliers, the market will allocate efficiently. Since all the conditions of free market competition are met with marginal benefit equal to marginal cost, the output is efficient (Figure 4.2).

FIGURE 4.2

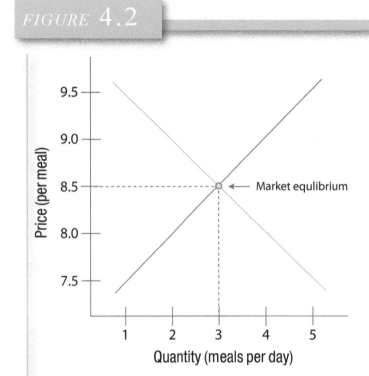

GRAPH OF SUPPLY AND DEMAND FOR LUNCH AT A FAST
FOOD RESTAURANT

WHAT IS AN EFFICIENT MARKET WITH SOCIAL CONSIDERATION?

Economists assume that in a market the societal demand is the sum of consumers' individual demand and the societal supply line is the sum of individual firms' supply.

Marginal Benefit and the Demand Line

Applying demand as a representation of value, each point on the consumer demand line is the amount of value relative to opportunity cost that consumers are willing to forgo of other consumption in order to gain more of a given product. Overall, the market demand line is the same as the societal demand line representing the value added, <u>marginal benefit</u>, at various prices (Figure 4.3).

FIGURE 4.3

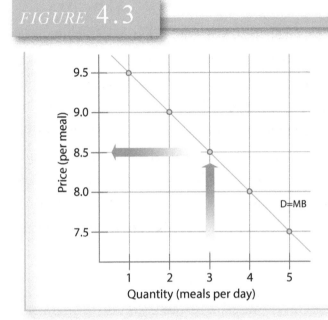

THE DEMAND LINE IS THE SOCIETAL MARGINAL BENEFIT

Marginal Cost and Supply Line Allocation

Representing supply as producer value, each point on the market supply line is the amount of value relative to opportunity cost that suppliers are willing to forgo of making other products. Overall, the market supply line is the same as the supply line for society. The marginal cost (value of opportunity cost) is shown as supply at various prices (Figure 4.4).

FIGURE 4.4

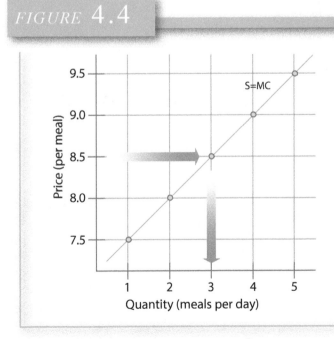

THE SUPPLY LINE IS THE SOCIETAL MARGINAL COST

The Principle Microeconomics Efficiency: MB=MC

The intercept of marginal benefit and marginal cost, MB=MC (Figure 4.5), is the societal market clearing price and market quantity of efficiency. At this point, the amount of additional benefit is equal to the additional cost. At no other point is efficiency and total satisfaction maximized. If MB is greater than MC, then additional costs are less than additional benefits and a higher quantity can be produced at less additional cost; thus inefficiency exists. By producing and consuming more, greater total satisfaction will occur until MB = MC. On the other hand, if MC is greater than MB, then additional benefits are less than additional costs. By producing and consuming less, greater satisfaction will occur until MC = MB. When competitive market equilibrium is achieved, marginal benefit equals marginal cost.

FIGURE 4.5

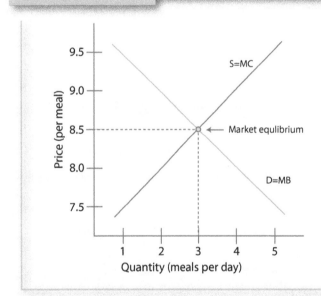

MARKET EQUILIBRIUM WITH SOCIAL BENEFITS: MB=MC

Inefficiency with Value Dynamics: Value versus Price

The market reflects varied individual values for a product. What happens when there is inefficiency because value and price are not the same for consumers and/or producers? For example, in our lunch allocation some consumers are willing to pay more for a lunch than the actual price in the market. These consumers value the product at more than the market price.

Likewise in our lunch example, some producers would be willing to produce for less than the price within the market. Let's review Table 4.2 to illustrate the economic impact of a price and value difference.

Traditional Supply and Demand Market Equilibrium

TABLE 4.3

	DEMAND AND SUPPLY TABLE OF CONSUMER AND PRODUCER VALUE FOR LUNCHES	
Quantity Demanded	Price	Quantity Supplied
0	$ 10.50	6
1	9.50	5
2	9.00	4
3	8.50	3
4	8.00	2
5	7.50	1
6	7.00	0

CONSUMER SURPLUS

When a consumer values the additional product (value added) at more than the price, a consumer surplus is present. The difference between value and price is the quantity of consumer surplus. In our example, notice that one person would be willing to pay $9.50 and another person would be willing to pay $9.00 since that is the value each additional consumer placed on the product. Only at equilibrium of $8.50 and a quantity of three is there an equality of price and value added.

CALCULATION OF CONSUMER SURPLUS

To calculate consumer surplus (Table 4.4), we recognize that one consumer would have been willing to buy the product at $9.50 or 1 unit more of satisfaction than the equilibrium price of $8.50 (9.5-8.5) and another consumer would have been willing to buy one additional lunch at $9 for .5 unit more of satisfaction (9.0-8.5). The total consumer surplus at $8.50 is 1 from the purchase value at $9.50 and .5 for the purchase value at $9.00 for a total consumer surplus of 1.5 at $8.50 (1. + .5).

TABLE 4.4

CONSUMER SURPLUS CALCULATION		
Price	Quantity Demanded	Consumer Surplus
$10.00	0	0
9.50	1 (1 additional)	9.5 - 8.5 = 1.0
9.00	2 (1 additional)	9.0 - 8.5 = .5
	Total Consumer Surplus @ $8.50	= 1.5

CALCULATION OF PRODUCER SURPLUS

For suppliers, the difference between supplier additional value and market price is producer surplus. In Table 4.5 one supplier would have been willing to produce the product at $7.50 or 1 unit more of producer satisfaction than equilibrium price of $8.50 (8.5 -7.5) and another supplier would have been willing to bring one additional lunch at $8.00 for .5 unit more of producer satisfaction (8.0-7.5). The total producer surplus at $8.50 is 1 from the purchase at $7.50 and .5 for the purchase at $8.0 for a total producer surplus of 1.5 (1+.5) at $8.50.

TABLE 4.5

CALCULATION OF PRODUCER SURPLUS		
Price	Quantity Supplied	Producer Surplus
$8.50	2 (1 additional)	8.5 - 8.0 = .5
7.50	1 (1 additional)	8.5 - 7.5 = 1.0
7.00	0	
	Total Consumer Surplus @ $8.50	= 1.5

Market Equilibrium

At $8.50, lunches produced and consumed provide a maximum level of both consumer and producer satisfaction. The market is in equilibrium at maximum satisfaction when there is no possible increase in total surplus for either consumers or producers at any other level of price/output. Consumers and producers each gain the largest surplus through the rationing forces of the market. The maximum satisfaction for consumers and producers is at 1.5 for consumer surplus plus 1.5 for producer surplus with a total surplus of 3 (1.5 +1.5) where MB=MC. The efficient allocation is graphically illustrated in Figure 4.6 as the darker blue area (consumer surplus) + the lighter area (producer surplus).

FIGURE 4.6

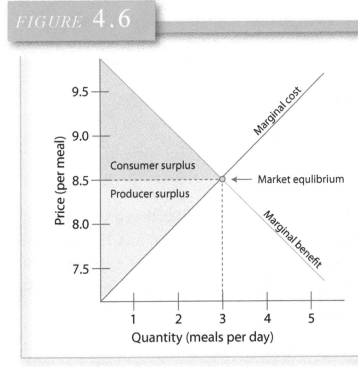

GRAPH OF EFFICIENT MARKET MB=MC

Measuring Inefficiency: Deadweight Loss

When costs are fully allocated for a good and benefits/costs are fully paid, market equilibrium will result with efficiency and maximum total consumer and producer surplus. However, when goods are allocated without full costs to the consumer/producer, the maximum total surplus is not realized, resulting in a market failure inefficiency. This disequilibrium is labeled a <u>deadweight loss</u>. Any price/output level other than equilibrium where MB=MC results in deadweight inefficiency.

If MB is greater than MC, as is the case with a price of $8.00, then under production is present and a deadweight loss is incurred in social benefit as shown in Figure 4.7. If more is produced to the point of MB=MC (by increasing output from two to three), the total surplus is increased and social benefit is increased.

FIGURE 4.7

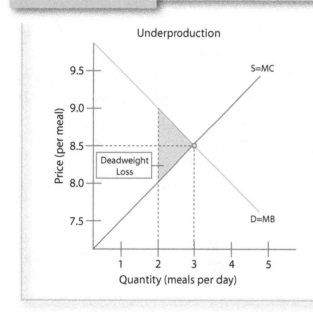

DEADWEIGHT LOSS WHEN MB>MC

If MC is greater than MB, as is the case with a price of $9.00, then over production is present and deadweight loss is incurred in social benefit as shown in Figure 4.8. Here if less is produced (by reducing quantity output from four to three; the point where MB=MC), the total surplus is increased for both consumers and producers. Social benefit is increased and efficiency is present by decreasing output.

FIGURE 4.8

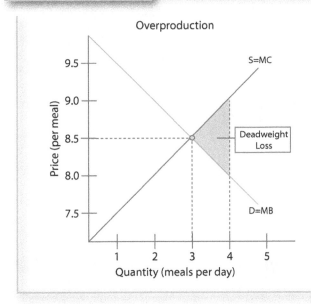

DEADWEIGHT LOSS WHEN MC>MB

Market Disequilibrium MB> or < than MC

A <u>market failure</u> exists when a resource allocation remains at a surplus or shortage position. When there is a shortage, inefficiency occurs due to the inability to increase output away from the under production. A surplus inefficiency occurs due to the inability to decrease output away from the over production. A temporary loss may be due to a short-term maladjustment in allocation that is corrected over time, but a longer-term condition is an ongoing market failure.

An example of a continuing deadweight loss is present when government mandates price controls (Figure 4.9). If government sets rent property prices below equilibrium, a price ceiling exists, and a deadweight loss results with marginal benefits greater than marginal costs due to under production. On the other hand, a price floor creates a deadweight loss as present with minimum wage legislation resulting where marginal costs are greater than marginal benefits, causing over production. In each instance government intervenes and market mechanisms are not allowed to efficiently ration output through price mechanisms of supply and demand.

FIGURE 4.9

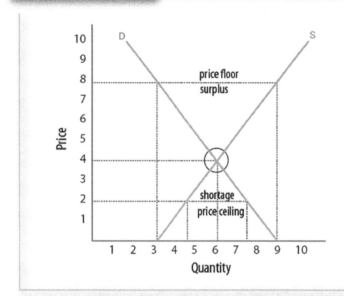

PRICE CEILING AND PRICE FLOOR SET BY GOVERNMENT

TYPES OF MARKET FAILURE

There are several types of market failures other than price ceilings and price floors. We now discuss some of the most prevalent failures including:

- Monopoly Power
- Externalities
- Government Regulation and Taxation
- Moral Hazard

Monopoly Power

The "invisible hand" of efficient allocation generally requires competition. When there is little or no competition in a market, monopoly power exists, often causing a higher price and a lower quantity of output. With lower output and higher prices, marginal benefits are greater than marginal costs and a deadweight cost accrues to society.

However, there are a few resource allocations where more competition does not meet efficiency and innovation economic goals. In such cases, government allows exceptions from competition. When a natural monopoly occurs or when a new product is marketed, government permits a sole supplier status.

A natural monopoly is a market where there are economies of scale, lower average costs (per unit costs) with increases in the quantity of output. By having only one producer in such a market, average costs will be lower than if several firms competed for the same market. For instance, this condition is present with city bus service. If there was more than one bus on each scheduled run, costs would push prices higher without any benefit to riders. Therefore, a city will grant monopoly status to one bus firm to reduce costs and prices.

Another exception to monopoly misallocation is present when government grants monopoly status to promote innovation. Patents and copyright laws exist so that inventors/writers can recoup their costs and profit from their product. Sole supplier status is granted to the inventor or writer but after a set period of time, the market for the product is restored to competition.

These cases of monopoly are granted exception by government; however, most monopoly applications result in a deadweight cost to society and total producer surpluses and consumer surpluses are lower than in a competitive market.

Market Externalities

Another type of market failure is labeled a <u>market externality</u>. Externalities exist in a market where third parties, not directly part of a transaction, are impacted by an economic transaction of two other parties. When externalities are present, the price does not fully reflect the total costs or total benefits of a transaction to all parties. Externalities involve what economists call spillover benefits and spillover costs. Spillovers benefits, labeled <u>merit goods</u>, increase the welfare of third parties while spillover costs, labeled <u>demerit goods,</u> decrease the welfare of third parties.

An example of a merit good is often cited in public expenditures for education. There is a direct payment made by society to schools, but often these economic outcomes result in greater benefits than the costs. Studies find that people educated by society are more likely to be employed, have a higher output because of increased skills, pay more taxes, and are less likely to be a future cost to society through welfare, health care, or prison costs.

A demerit good is present when production or consumption inflicts costs on third parties not part of a market transaction. An example is pollution caused by automobiles. Individuals driving automobiles gain by having transportation and the automobile manufacturer/oil industry gains by the sale, but third parties that are not part of this transaction, are given the by-product cost of air pollution and traffic congestion. Therefore, the total economic cost of driving the car is not included in the prices paid by users.

Corrections for Misallocation of Resources within Market Failures

Government can reallocate resources when negative or positive externalities impact the economic system. Government attempts to correct or lessen negative externalities of pollution through regulation, taxes, and fines. For example, higher taxes on cars emitting higher levels of pollution will increase prices of these cars and decrease the quantity sold. Consumers will then buy cheaper, lower-pollution-emitting cars and less total pollution will result. Regulation may also be imposed directly to decrease pollution. A combination of regulation and increased costs were used to decrease automobile pollution by requiring catalytic converters on all cars driven in the United States. These converters increased costs to manufacturers and prices to consumers. Therefore, there was a decrease in the supply schedule due to the extra cost at every price and a decrease in quantity demanded with the increased cost for consumers. The cost to third parties for pollution decreased as pollution was reduced with less pollution per car and fewer cars on the road.

FIGURE 4.10

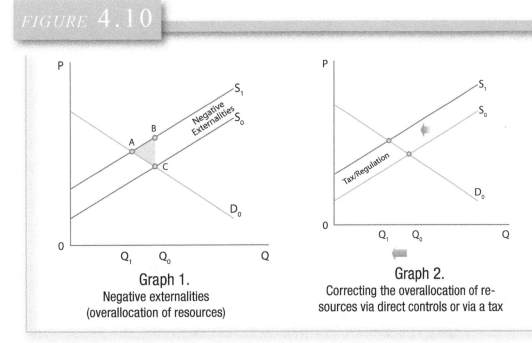

Graph 1.
Negative externalities
(overallocation of resources)

Graph 2.
Correcting the overallocation of resources via direct controls or via a tax

THE REALLOCATION TO INTERNALIZE DEMERIT COSTS TO CONSUMERS OR PRODUCERS BY TAXES OR REGULATION

Regulation

The reallocation to internalize the costs of a demerit good to consumers and producers is illustrated in Figure 4.10. There is a deadweight cost of over production as shown in the A, B, and C triangle of Graph 1 that is reallocated in Graph 2 by decreasing the supply line from S_0 to S_1 in Graph 2 with quantity decreasing from Q_0, to Q_1. Government regulation or taxes decreases supply and increases prices. The decreased quantity reduces the demerit externality.

When merit goods are produced, marginal benefits are greater than marginal costs and public well-being can be increased by granting subsidies to either consumers or suppliers for increased output. Through this process, the benefits of merit are internalized into greater production.

The reallocation to internalize the benefits of a merit good is illustrated in Figure 4.11. In Graph 1 supply = demand and is in equilibrium at quantity Q_0, but a deadweight loss of under production exists as shown in triangle A,B,C. With an increase in demand from D_0 to D_1 as shown in Graph 2, or an increase in supply from S_0 to S_1 as shown in Graph 3, output increases to Q_1 from Q_0. The deadweight loss triangle in Graph 1 is resolved by either increasing the demand (Graph 2) or increasing the supply (Graph 3) each resulting in more output. By increasing output, an additional value is added for society, eliminating the market deadweight loss.

FIGURE 4.11

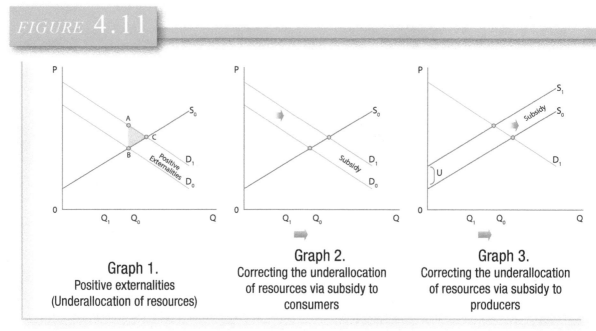

Graph 1.
Positive externalities
(Underallocation of resources)

Graph 2.
Correcting the underallocation
of resources via subsidy to
consumers

Graph 3.
Correcting the underallocation
of resources via subsidy to
producers

THE REALLOCATION TO INTERNALIZE DEMERIT COSTS TO
CONSUMERS OR PRODUCERS BY TAXES OR REGULATION

Moral Hazard

Moral hazard is another form of negative externality. This market failure is created by individuals assuming an economic risk that is shifted to others. A moral hazard is present whenever risks are individually undertaken, but potential economic losses are transferred to another party. Within the health industry negative externalities are present when an individual chooses to smoke cigarettes or drink alcohol in excess. Although the result is generally a decrease in the health of individuals, the economic cost of medical care is often transferred to the public through insurance or public hospital care. When the economic cost of the externality of risky behavior is borne by others, a <u>moral hazard</u> exists.

The cost of a moral hazard was incurred on a large macroeconomic basis in 2007 due to dramatic losses in the subprime residential loan market. These market losses were caused by some bankers who made short-term profitable loans knowing the loans were unlikely to be repaid. When the loans resulted in foreclosure of the homes, the government assumed much of the economic loss to avoid a larger macro problem. These losses would not have been incurred if bankers individually would have been responsible for their decisions.

THE ALLOCATION OF PUBLIC GOODS

There are other allocations in our economy without the competition of the market system to ensure efficiency against market failure. Market failures are often cited in public expenditures because of the nature of this allocation. Since public expenditures are not rationed by the forces of supply and demand, most government goods cannot be allocated through a competitive market system. Unlike private goods, public goods have the economic characteristic of non-excludability and non-rivalry. Non-excludability means that the goods are available to all people without exclusion of any person. Non-rivalry means that the allocation is without competition.

Many public goods cannot be produced in a private market system because costs cannot be paid by people receiving the benefits or there is insufficient profit from the production. A lighthouse is an illustration of a public good that is both non-excludable and non-rival in production. Any ship in the area can benefit from the light warning, but private firms cannot sell the service because no market can be established to bill beneficiaries.

Private goods are exclusive and in a competitive market, meaning goods are produced with rivalry and only available to those who pay for benefits. For example, a country club is a private good in a competitive market where only members are allowed to participate. Such a private good is within a market allocation of rivalry and excludability.

Most public goods are outside of market forces. Public expenditures are largely non-excludable such as national defense, and many other public costs are non-rival such as public health, transportation, and security services. A large amount of public funds are spent on nonmarket transfer payments alone. Because of the non-rivalry and non-excludability nature of public goods production, efficiency is a challenge, but the theory of allocation remains relevant. If marginal benefits exceed marginal costs, an economic action can be undertaken for additional satisfaction for society.

© Makarova Viktoria, 2013. Used under license from Shutterstock, Inc.

A Merit Good Allocation Problem: The Free Rider

When public funds are used to enhance a positive externality, there may be a resulting economic problem called the <u>free rider principle</u>. Some merit goods provide benefits selectively without cost to beneficiaries. In this case some individuals gain from the public production of a good, but they do not incur any or only a small portion of the cost compared to their individual benefit received. The obvious example of a free rider application is when someone literally rides for free on public transportation while others pay for the service. Further examples exist when any public expenditure grants a greater value to some individuals than to the public in general. Examples include roads built to seldom used areas or even public art displays or services unique to a neighborhood benefitting local residents. The question of whether government should pay for such projects should be based upon the marginal benefit to society versus the marginal cost.

When Should Government Pay?

Public expenditures by their nature are subject to debate because they are non-excludable and non-rival. The challenge of public expenditures is to assure allocation according to economic principles. Marginal costs must be analyzed both accurately and fully. What services actually marginally benefit the "greater good" more than their marginal cost?

We know when there is efficiency in a competitive market, the costs and benefits require that the full costs and full prices are a part of the efficient allocation, but with public goods production there often is no competitive market.

Micro Theory and the Allocation of Public Expenditures

The microeconomic theory of allocation applies not only to the private sector output but to all economic activity. The principle of microeconomics theorizes that output is justified as long as the marginal benefits are greater than or equal to marginal costs. A low cost of government is not the economic goal for public expenditures, but rather, maximum utility for individuals and society. A project should be undertaken as long as its value added is greater than its added cost.

The problem of applying this theory is one of measurement. How do we measure the benefits of a public hospital or disease prevention? What is the benefit of national defense or pollution regulation? Our goal in most allocations is not the complete eradication of loss or even elimination of risk, but rather a balance of expenditure with benefit. Even with pollution abatement, regulation, and taxation or internalization of pollution costs, government intervention should be taken not to completely eliminate pollution, but rather to promote balanced economic sustainability, encouraging efficiency, full employment, and if possible, full marginal costs to beneficiaries. Some amount of pollution is inevitable and even sustainable, but a logical allocation balance of resources is the goal.

GOVERNMENT AND MARKET FAILURE

There is a market failure debate among economists about the appropriateness of government expenditures and intervention. Some economists argue that free market forces left alone will reallocate better than government. The Coase Theory suggests that a free market will ultimately realign itself better than government. When a market failure exists, at certain times free market forces can result in all parties of an economic production cooperating to reallocate for the benefit of each individual without government. For instance, beekeepers, consumers, and farmers each can benefit from working together. Farmers benefit from bee pollination, beekeepers from honey, and consumers from crops as well as honey. In a market arrangement without government, it is likely that farmers will negotiate with beekeepers to benefit consumers, beekeepers, and themselves. Free market advocates exemplified by the Austrian School of Economics, supply side advocates, and followers of noted economist Milton Friedman, argue that government intervention has added costs without allowing adjustments for cooperative market forces. Government may sometimes promote greater inefficiency than a market left unhampered.

When Should Government Produce Public Goods and/ or Intervene in Market Failures?

Most economists support production of some public goods such as national defense and many economists agree with government market intervention in some market failures, but there is a controversy as to the extent and means of intervention. Given disequilibrium between marginal benefits and marginal costs, in theory there is economic gain when government lessens deadweight market failures. Through the use of government actions, if the marginal individual and social benefits exceed the marginal individual and social costs, greater government action is justified but the assumptions and measurements must be economically of merit.

CONCLUSION: PUBLIC WORKS AND MARKET FORCES

Market failures are a reality with capitalism. A social balance of private and public allocation promotes the highest and best use of resources and results in maximum utility for individuals and society. The actions of government can create too much regulation, taxation, or subsidization resulting in under production on the one hand and inefficiency and over production on the other, and result in over production. Government production of public goods/services is less likely to be competitively adjusted through the market place. But the principle of microeconomic theory applies to both public and private allocations. When consumer and producer surplus is maximized, individuals and society will gain maximum satisfaction as well.

Deadweight Loss is a positive externality is a market loss causing over or under allocation.

Efficiency occurs when resources are allocated for maximum benefit to individuals and society.

Externality, Negative: (Demerit Good): A negative externality is a market failure due to over allocation when full price is not paid by consumer and/or producer but a cost is shifted to a third party not part of a transaction such as pollution of a factory.

Externality, Positive: (Merit Good): A positive externality is a market failure due to under allocation when the market produces less than the most desirable output because total benefits are not included in the market price such as in education allocation where subsidies are often given by government to increase output.

Moral Hazard exists when individuals assume greater risks because losses in part or total are shifted to third parties.

Market Failure is a situation in which there is inefficient allocation of resources within the market.

Natural Monopoly is a market with extensive economies of scale where average total cost declines with increases in output.

Pareto Optimality is the theoretical maximum utility allocation resulting in maximum total surplus without sacrifice to any individual.

Surplus, Consumer is the difference between consumer individual marginal benefit and price.

Surplus, Producer is the difference between producer marginal benefit and price.

Surplus, Total is the sum of consumer and producer surplus.

Value and Price: Value is the marginal expected benefit from an additional purchase for a consumer or the marginal expected benefit for a supplier from an additional output. Price is the equilibrium market clearing price within the market.

APPLIED EXERCISES:

EXERCISE 1 :

Assume a State Government has the following successive options for public investments given the benefits and costs as noted.

PROJECT	COST	BENEFIT
A	$100	$200
B	300	800
C	600	1,300
D	1,000	1,600
E	1,500	1,900

A: Which, if any, projects should be undertaken? Why?

B: Should Project E be undertaken? Why or why not?

EXERCISE 2 :

QUANTITY DEMANDED	PRICE	QUANTITY SUPPLIED
10	$60	50
20	50	40
30	40	30
40	30	20
50	20	10

A: Given the above Supply and Demand Schedules, what is the most efficient allocation?

B: What is the consumer surplus at a price of $40?

C: What is the producer surplus at a price of $40?

D: What is the maximum total surplus for this allocation?

APPLIED EXERCISES: ANSWERS

EXERCISE 1:

Assume a State Government has the following options for public investments given the benefits and costs as noted.

PROJECT	COST	BENEFIT	MARGINAL COST	MARGINAL BENEFIT
A	$100	$200		
			100	600
B	300	800		
			300	500
C	600	1,300		
			400	300
D	1,000	1,600		
			500	300
E	1,500	1,900		

A. Which, if any, projects should be undertaken? Why?

Projects A, B and C allow a greater marginal benefit than marginal cost, therefore they should be undertaken, but not Projects D and E.

B. Should Project E be undertaken? Why or why not?

No, because the marginal cost for Project E is $500 and the marginal benefit is only $300.

EXERCISE 2 :

Quantity Demanded	Price	Quantity Supplied
10	$60	50
20	50	40
30	40	30
40	30	20
50	20	10

A. **Given the above Supply and Demand Schedules, what is the most efficient allocation?**

Quantity Demanded equals Quantity Supplied at a Price = $40 and Quantity = 30.

B. **What is the consumer surplus at a price of $40?**

To calculate consumer surplus, we recognize that 10 consumers would have bought at $60 rather than $40 meaning there is a surplus of (60 − 40) = 20 × 10 or 200 surplus. 10 consumers would have bought at $50 rather than $40 meaning there is a surplus of (60 − 50) × 10 or 100. Total consumer surplus is therefore 200 + 100 or 300.

C. **What is the producer surplus at a price of $40?**

To calculate producer surplus, we recognize that 20 fewer units are sold at $20 for a producer surplus of 200 ($20 × 10) and 10 fewer at $40 − $30 for a surplus of ($10 × 10) for a surplus of 100. Total producer surplus is 200 + 100 for 300.

D. **What is the maximum total surplus for this allocation?**

The total consumer surplus + producer surplus is the total surplus or a value of 300 + 300 = 600.

ELASTICITY
AND ALLOCATION

ELASTICITY AS A PRIMARY ENDOGENOUS VARIABLE

Microeconomic analysis centers on the role of the firm or consumer and choices that can be made to improve performance given the macroeconomic environment. In Lesson 3 supply and demand factors of allocation were discussed noting the resultant equilibrium price and quantity for a product.

Supply and demand is defined by price and quantity but elasticity defines the response to a change in price along a supply or demand line.

An **elasticity of demand coefficient** measures the percentage change in quantity purchased compared to the percentage change in price.

An **elasticity of supply coefficient** measures the percentage change in quantity supplied compared to the percentage change in price.

All consumers and suppliers are elastic (sensitive) to large price changes but for analysis economists assume a moderate price change.

LEARNING OBJECTIVES

Please note the listed objectives. As you will see, the course materials are all objective driven. This provides you with a constant way to direct and monitor your progress throughout the course.

1 OBJECTIVE ONE

Demonstrate an understanding of elasticity of supply and elasticity of demand.

2 OBJECTIVE TWO

Use the total revenue approach to distinguish elastic from inelastic business situations.

3 OBJECTIVE THREE

Apply the midpoint formula to determine the coefficient of elasticity and its impact in business.

4 OBJECTIVE FOUR

Identify and describe the determinates of elasticity of supply and the elasticity of demand.

5 OBJECTIVE FIVE

Describe the effects of time and government regulation on the relative elasticity of a transaction.

I INTERACTIVE EXERCISE

Explain the concepts of income elasticity and cross-elasticity.

Types of demand elasticity

Elastic demand is a sensitive response by consumers to price changes. With an elastic price change to quantity demanded, the percentage change in quantity is greater than the percentage change in price. Consumers are elastic (sensitive) to changes in the price of used clothing or used automobiles. Price increases with elastic demand will cause a decrease in total revenue.

Inelastic demand is an insensitive response by consumers to price changes. With an inelastic price change to quantity demanded, the percentage change in quantity is less than the percentage change in price. Price increases with inelastic demand will cause an increase in total revenue. Consumers are generally inelastic to changes in medical and gasoline prices within a moderate price change.

Unitary elasticity of demand occurs when the total revenue remains the same whether a price is increased or decreased. Demand is unitary when there is a proportional (inverse proportionality) change in both quantity and price. With unitary demand, producers may charge either a higher or lower price but the total revenue will remain the same.

Graphic Representations of Perfectly Elastic

Perfectly elastic and **perfectly inelastic graphs** are represented by a straight line. When a relationship is perfectly elastic, the percentage change in quantity is infinite and the coefficient of elasticity is infinite with any change in price. Perfectly inelastic is when the percentage change in quantity is zero, meaning there is no change in quantity with a change in price. Perfectly elastic demand is infinitely sensitive to a change in price while perfectly inelastic demand is totally non-responsive to changes in price. A perfectly elastic demand line is horizontal and a perfectly inelastic demand line is vertical.

FIGURE 5.1

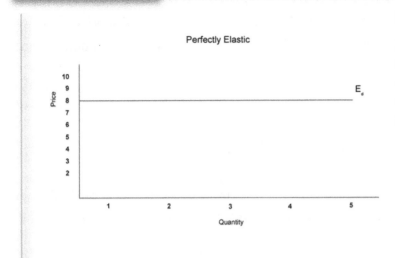

Perfectly elastic demand line

In a perfectly elastic graph a small change in price will cause an infinite change in quantity demanded because the line is horizontal.

FIGURE 5.2

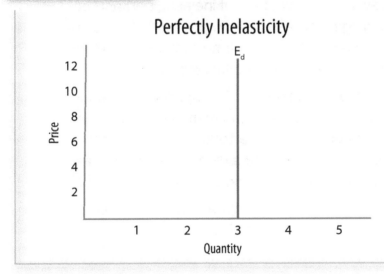

Perfectly inelastic demand line

Perfectly inelastic demand occurs when a change in price results in no change in quantity demanded.

In perfectly inelastic demand the total revenue declines as the price drops because a lower price with a constant quantity results in lower total revenue (price times quantity = total revenue). In Figure 5.2 the quantity remains at three and the price declines from $12 to $2, therefore total revenue decreases from $36 to $6.

A Perfectly Elastic Coefficient = Infinity
A Perfectly Inelastic Coefficient = zero

Measures of Elasticity of Demand

There are two ways of measuring price elasticity: 1) the total revenue test and 2) the coefficient of elasticity (midpoint formula). Each method will determine if a price change is elastic or inelastic but only the coefficient of elasticity will measure the amount of elasticity (sensitivity).

The total revenue approach applied

The total revenue method is the easiest calculation of price elasticity. This method determines elasticity by comparing the direction of price change with the direction of total revenue change.

- If the price and total revenue change in the same direction, price is inelastic (insensitive). When businesses increase prices and consumers are inelastic to the price increase, total revenue increases. Businesses assume an inelastic demand when they increase prices to raise total revenue. An example of inelastic demand occurs when a public college increases tuition prices. Colleges are assuming an inelastic demand, therefore an increase in tuition rates generally results in an increase in total revenue.

- If the price and total revenue change in the opposite direction, price is elastic (sensitive). Businesses assume an elastic demand when they decrease prices to increase total revenue. Because consumers are sensitive to the price of airline travel, a decrease in the ticket price will often result in an increase in total revenue.

- If the total revenue remains the same with a change in price either up or down, price has unitary elasticity.

TABLE 5.1

Price	Quantity Demanded	Total Revenue	Elasticity
$10	1	10	
9	2	18	Elastic
8	3	24	Elastic
7	4	28	Elastic
6	5	30	Elastic
5	6	30	Unitary
4	7	28	Inelastic

A Total Revenue Elasticity Application

The total revenue test is applied in the table above. On all decreases in price from $10 to $6, the total revenue increases and therefore the consumers are elastic (sensitive) to price change. From $6 to $5 the total revenue remains the same resulting in unitary elasticity. The price change from $5 to $4 results in a decrease in total revenue and the consumers become inelastic to price change. A firm would not produce in the inelastic segment of the market because with a drop in price, total revenue also decreases.

THE COEFFICIENT OF ELASTICITY OF DEMAND

The degree of price elasticity of demand is calculated using the **midpoint formula** to find the **coefficient of elasticity**. The amount of change in quantity is divided by the midpoint (average) of the two quantities in the numerator divided by the amount of change in price divided by the midpoint of the two prices in the denominator. The coefficient is characterized as a positive value for simplicity purposes. However, there is an inverse relationship between price and quantity demanded. Figure 5.3 illustrates calculation of demand elasticity by both the coefficient and total revenue approaches.

The Coefficient of Price Demand Elasticity is a quantitative measure of responsiveness. The coefficient of price elasticity of demand compares the amount of change in quantity ($Q_1 - Q_2$) from a midpoint of two quantities (($Q_1 + Q_2$)/2) in the numerator to the amount of change in price ($P_1 - P_2$) from a midpoint of two prices (($P_1 + P_2$)/2) in the denominator. This formula measures the amount of change in quantity divided by the average quantity (midpoint) divided by the amount of change in price divided by the average price (midpoint).

$$\text{Elasticity of Demand} = \frac{\dfrac{\text{Change in quantity demanded of X}}{\text{Average quantity of X}}}{\dfrac{\text{Change in price of X}}{\text{Average Price of X}}}$$

$$\text{Elasticity of Demand} = \frac{\text{\% Change in quantity demanded}}{\text{\% Change in price}}$$

When the demand is price elastic, the percentage change in quantity exceeds the percentage change in price. The value of the coefficient is therefore greater than 1 and the larger the value, the greater the price elasticity. A value of 1.2 is considered sensitive to price while a value of 2.5 very sensitive.

When the price is price inelastic, the percentage change in quantity is less than the percentage change in price. The value of the coefficient is therefore less than 1 (a decimal) and the smaller the value, the less the sensitivity to price change. A value of 0.6 is considered insensitive while a value of 0.1 is very insensitive.

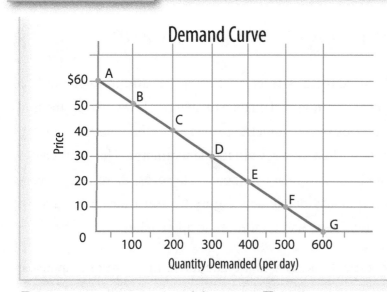

FIGURE 5.3

DEMAND LINE WITH VARIED ELASTICITY

TABLE 5.2

(1) Price	(2) Quantity	(3) Elasticity	(4) Total Revenue (1) x (2)	Total Revenue Test
$60	0		$0	
		← 11.0		← Elastic
50	100		5000	
		← 3.0		← Elastic
40	200		8000	
		← 1.4		← Elastic
30	300		9000	
		← .7		← Inelastic
20	400		8000	
		← .3		← Inelastic
10	500		5000	

Note that the changes in price and quantity in the elasticity formula are absolute values as the result will be the same regardless of the direction of price and quantity change; therefore, it is easier to subtract the smaller number from the larger in applying the formula.

In Figure 5.3, the elasticity can be calculated as shown in Table 5.2 for each of the points A through G. From point B to C the quantity changed from 100 at $50 to 200 at $40. Therefore, in the numerator, the change in quantity is 100 over the average quantity (100 + 200) / 2 = 150 and in the denominator the change in price is $10, from $50 to $40, over the average price ($50 + $40)/2 = $45. This results in 100/150 over 10/45, (invert and multiply) (100/150 × 45/10) = (4,500/1,500) = 3. An elasticity coefficient of three is price elastic a price change from $50 to $40.

Price Elasticity Along a Demand Line

Prices are more elastic at the upper end of a demand line as in Figure 5.3. When applied to the formula, the quantities are smaller at higher prices and therefore, the percentage change in quantity is larger than the percentage change in price. The numerator in the elasticity formula is larger than the denominator resulting in a higher coefficient.

Estimated Price Elasticity of Demand for Various Goods

Product	Estimated Ed
Salt	.1
Coffee	.3
Doctor Services	.6
Private Education	1.1
Restaurant Meals	2.3
Airline Travel (long-run)	2.4
Foreign Travel (long-run)	4.0

The above data was derived by many studies. Consumers are inelastic to changes in the price of salt but very elastic to the long-run change in price of foreign travel. There is a relatively unitary relationship between increases in the cost of private education and quantity demanded.

An Economic Application of Price Elasticity Coefficient

A price elasticity coefficient describes the expected change in quantity demanded with a 1% change in price. With a coefficient of elasticity of Ed = 1.7, then a 1% increase in price will yield a 1.7% decrease in quantity demanded. The coefficient value is elastic because it is greater than 1 but in the opposite direction of price change. The value of price elasticity as determined through the midpoint system will have a positive sign (+) as it is an absolute value but it may be less than 1 (a decimal).

Example: If the coefficient of elasticity of demand is 2, how is quantity demanded impacted by a 5% increase in price?

- A 1% increase in price would decrease quantity by 2%

  $[(E_d) = $ 2% change in quantity / 1% change in price];
- Therefore, a 5% increase in price will decrease quantity by (2 × 5) or 10%.

  $[(E_d) = $ 10% change in quantity / 5% change in price]

The determinants of elasticity of demand

- The most important determinant of elasticity is the availability of substitutes. Products with many substitutes will be elastic.

  Example: You choose from many alternatives for fast food restaurants so the quantity demanded tends to be sensitive to price changes (i.e., 99 cent offerings on a menu)

- Another determinant is whether the good/service is a luxury or a necessity. Goods/services that are a luxury are not a required purchase and therefore are more sensitive to price changes.

  Example: An individual may purchase a plane ticket for a weekend vacation if the cost is low. Luxury items by definition are purchased as an extra, something you do not need to buy.

By contrast a necessity such as medical care is inelastic to price. Individuals are not sensitive to price changes when the item is a necessity and not an option. (An unusual application is found in the purchase of an expensive automobile. An expensive automobile purchased by a wealthy individual is viewed as a necessity by that individual and not a luxury. Therefore, it is often inelastic to price change.)

- The percentage of the total budget spent on goods/services is also a determinant of elasticity. When a large percentage of the budget is spent on an item, the item is price elastic and when a small percentage of the budget is spent on an item, it is inelastic.

Example: You may be sensitive to the price of a new home but inelastic to the price change of salt.

- Time is a determinant of elasticity. The amount of time a consumer spends shopping can be compared to price changes. When a consumer spends much time shopping for a "good price" they are price sensitive but may be time insensitive.

Examples: a shopper at a convenience store is time sensitive but price insensitive while a coupon purchaser is price sensitive but time insensitive.

- A final application of price sensitivity is in the amount of time needed to adjust to a price change. If gasoline prices increase substantially, you might continue to purchase the same amount in the short term, but in the long term you will purchase a more gasoline efficient car. Therefore you are price inelastic now but price elastic for the future.

Practical Applications of Elasticity

Farm produce tends to be inelastic to price changes. The real price (price adjusted for inflation) of eggs is much less today than 50 years ago but consumers are insensitive to the price decrease, thereby spending less per person on eggs today than 50 years ago.

The application of excise taxes (taxes charged by the state or federal government for the purchase of a good) varies in price sensitivity. In 1992 federal tax increases were imposed on yachts, but luxury consumers were actually price sensitive and total revenue decreased with increases in prices. In contrast, gasoline taxes were also increased by $.05 per gallon; however, price was inelastic as the total spent on gasoline increased. Government seeks to impose excise taxes on inelastic prices to raise revenue.

Illegal drugs are often considered price inelastic by consumers. Because of the relationship of illegal drug purchases to acts of crime, there are varied views on how society can best deal with this problem. If consumers of illegal drugs are inelastic to price changes, a decreased supply of illegal drugs would increase prices that could result in more crime being committed by drug addicts to make purchases. Others argue that a decrease in supply will decrease availability and result in less use.

Minimum wage increases are often considered price elastic. If wages are increased by a government mandate, then the total spent on wages by firms would go down and fewer workers would be employed.

Concept Summary of Price Elasticity Coefficient and Total Revenue Approaches

TABLE 5.3

Demand Elasticity	Elasticity Coefficient	Change in Price	Total Revenue Direction
Elastic	ED > 1	Increase	Decrease
Elastic	ED > 1	Decrease	Increase
Unitary	ED = 1	Increase or Decrease	No Change
Inelastic	ED < 1	Increase	Increase
Inelastic	ED < 1	Decrease	Decrease

Elasticity of Supply: Producer Elasticity to Price Changes

Price elasticity of supply is the sensitivity of producers to changes in price. The supply elasticity formula is similar to demand elasticity but applied to changes in the quantity supplied with changes in price. When the elasticity of supply coefficient is greater than one, producers are sensitive to price changes and will increase the percentage of quantity supplied more than the percentage increase in price. If the elasticity of supply coefficient is less than one, producers are insensitive to price changes and will increase the percentage of quantity supplied less than the percentage increase in price.

$$\text{Supply Elasticity} = \frac{\%\ \text{Change in quantity supplied}}{\%\ \text{Change in price}}$$

$$\text{Supply Elasticity} = \frac{\dfrac{\text{Change in quantity supplied of X}}{\text{Average quantity of X}}}{\dfrac{\text{Change in price of X}}{\text{Average Price of X}}}$$

Determinants of Elasticity of Supply

The elasticity of supply coefficient is dependent upon the amount of time producers have to adjust quantity supplied with price change. An increase in the time for suppliers to respond will result in greater elasticity. There are three possible time frames for a supplier: the market period (immediate time frame with no change in output possible), the short-run or intermediate period (sufficient time to change to capacity), and the long-run (all factors of production are changeable).

The market period is the immediate market time frame. Elasticity of supply is inelastic (supply line is vertical) as no quantity adjustments can be made immediately. Consider a melon farmer when the crop will mature within a week and market demand increases. The farmer cannot change quantity supplied by planting more melons but the farmer can ration existing supply by raising price as in Figure 5.4. The price will rise from P1 to P2 with an increase in demand from D1 to D2 and with no increase in quantity.

FIGURE 5.4

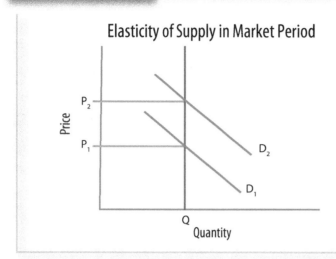

The **short-run period** or intermediate period is a time period such that the producer can increase to capacity but cannot increase capacity. This elasticity coefficient of supply is relatively elastic. For example, consider a widget factory that experiences an increase in demand for their product. In the short run the factory can increase to capacity by operating 24 hours per day and seven days a week but cannot build a new factory.

TIME FRAMES FOR A SUPPLIER

Market period short-run period long-run period

With an increase in demand from D_1 to D_2 both price (P_1 to P_2) and quantity (Q_1 to Q_2) will increase.

FIGURE 5.5

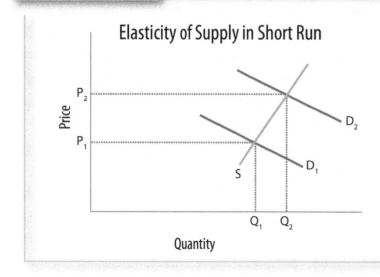

The **long-run period** is defined as a time period with no fixed factors of production (land, labor, capital and entrepreneurship). In the long run all factors of production can be altered to increase or decrease capacity. The elasticity of supply in long run is elastic given no restraints on resources. An example of this principle is a movement from the short-run period to the long run when a firm moves to a larger plant and increases all input resources to increase output.

There is a substantial potential increase in quantity and increase in price with a long-run adjustment. The amount of price elasticity depends upon the resource price of inputs.

FIGURE 5.6

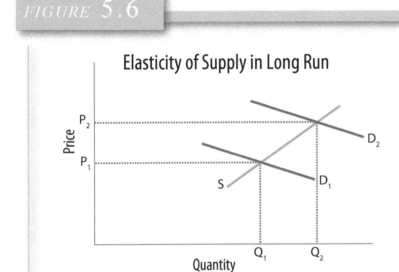

PRICE SENSITIVITY TO GOVERNMENT SET PRICES: PRICE CEILING

When government sets a legal price ceiling (price below equilibrium price) or a legal price floor (price above equilibrium), the sensitivity by consumers and producers determines the amount of surplus or shortage that results.

A price ceiling is the maximum legal price a seller may charge for a product or service. The price ceiling is set below price equilibrium to keep prices below where quantity demanded equals quantity supplied. When consumers and producers are elastic (sensitive) to price, the result will be a shortage. Consumers are elastic to price and will want more quantity at that price, however, producers are also elastic to price and will produce less. See Figure 5.7.

Examples: Rent controls and credit card interest ceilings.

FIGURE 5.7

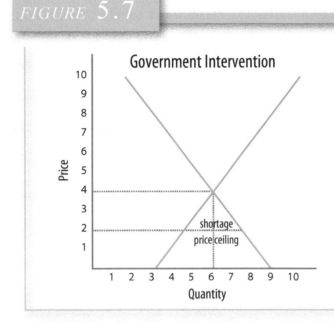

Legal Price Floor

A price floor is the minimum price fixed by government. Price floors are set to increase prices for suppliers of resources. When government sets a price floor (price above equilibrium price) and both consumers and producers are elastic (sensitive) to price, the result will be a large surplus. Consumers are elastic to price and will buy less at that price, however, producers are also elastic and will produce more.

Examples of this process include minimum-wage legislation and farm price supports. The surplus resulting is related to demand and supply elasticity. When both the supply of workers and the demand for workers is sensitive, fewer workers will be employed. More workers will be willing to work, however employers will employ fewer workers (see Figure 5.8).

FIGURE 5.8

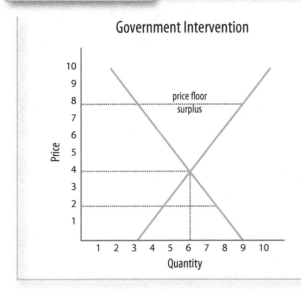

OTHER PRICE SENSITIVITIES

Economists use two other measures of elasticity: income elasticity and cross elasticity.

Income elasticity is the sensitivity of quantity demanded of good to a change in income. This coefficient quantifies whether a good is an inferior or superior good and the degree of income sensitivity.

$$\text{Income Elasticity Coeffcient} = \frac{\text{\% Change in quantity demanded of product X}}{\text{\% Change in income}}$$

For **superior** or **normal good** consumers will increase their demand with an increase in income. A superior good will have a coefficient of income elasticity greater than 0 (the higher the value, the stronger the sensitivity).

Examples include purchases of yachts or new cars; the coefficient of income elasticity > 0.

Inferior goods have a negative coefficient of income elasticity, therefore the greater the income, the lower the quantity demanded response. Inferior goods have a coefficient of income elasticity less than 0 (the larger the negative, the stronger the inferiority).

Examples include purchase of beans or used clothing, the coefficient of income elasticity < 0.

Cross elasticity of demand is the sensitivity of the change in the quantity demanded of a good to the change in price of another good. This calculation tests the degree and type of relationship between two products. A positive cross elasticity coefficient such as 2 is a substitute relationship while a negative coefficient such as −2 would note a complementary relationship.

$$\text{Cross Elasticity Coeffcient} = \frac{\text{\% Change in quantity demanded of product X}}{\text{\% Change in price of product Y}}$$

Complementary goods are purchased together and have a less than 0 coefficient (negative value).

Examples include digital cameras and memory sticks where the coefficient of cross elasticity <0 since the two products are sold together.

Substitute goods are purchased in place of one another and the coefficient of cross elasticity is greater than 0 meaning the items are substitutes.

Example: Sweet'N Low and NutraSweet are substitutes and the coefficient of cross elasticity is > 0.

In Conclusion

There are many economic measures for analyzing consumer and producer sensitivity to price, income, and prices of related goods. Each of these measurements describes the options that a firm has in meeting consumer demand.

REAL WORLD ECONOMICS

HOW AND WHEN ARE CONSUMERS ELASTIC TO GASOLINE PRICES?

The price elasticity of gasoline is varied along a demand line as described by economic theory. As expected, consumers are more elastic at higher prices when consumers are more likely to substitute alternative means of transportation.

When gasoline prices are high, there is also a difference in consumer price elasticity between decreases and increases in prices. According to one study, at high prices consumers are more sensitive to price increases than they are to price decreases.

"During times of rising oil prices, consumers are very price conscious and shop for deals . . .

When oil prices go down, however, consumers are less alert to prices and compare much less as long as they see even a small price reduction. This allows gasoline retailers to lower prices at a slower pace as they recover some of the profit margins lost on the way up."

www.blogginstocks.com

Coefficient of Price Elasticity is a measure of consumer price sensitivity found by dividing the percentage change in quantity/the midpoint quantity in the numerator by the percentage change in price/the midpoint price in the denominator. If the resulting absolute value is greater than 1 it is elastic, and if less than 1 it is inelastic.

Cross Elasticity of Demand is a measure of price sensitivity between products quantifying the change in the price of one good/service to a change in the quantity demanded of another good/service. If the resulting value is positive, there is a substitute relationship between the variables, however if the value is negative, there is a complementary relationship.

Exogenous/Endogenous Variables: Exogenous variables are external to the operation of a firm or consumer such as the macroeconomic conditions. Endogenous variables are internal to the operation of a firm or consumer and relate to adjustments to costs and revenue for a firm or income for a consumer.

Income Elasticity of Demand is a measure of sensitivity of demand for a good/service to a change in income. If the resulting value is positive, the good/service is a superior good but if the value is negative, the good/service is an inferior good.

Market Period/Short Run/Long Run on Elasticity of Supply: The elasticity of supply is sensitive to the amount of time producers have to change their output. In the immediate market period, there is no time to adjust so supply is inelastic to price, however, it becomes more elastic with greater time. In the short run, the supply is relatively elastic and even more elastic in the long run.

Price Elasticity of Demand is a measure of the sensitivity of consumers to changes in prices.

Price Ceiling is a mandatory price set by government below market price equilibrium generally resulting in a shortage.

Price Floor: Macroeconomics is a study of the total economy or large sectors of the overall national economy.

Perfectly Elastic: Perfectly elastic demand is a horizontal line and any change in price results in an infinite change in quantity demanded. Perfectly inelastic demand is a vertical line illustrating no change in quantity demanded.

Price Elasticity of Supply is a measure of price sensitivity by producers to a change in price.

Total Revenue Test of Elasticity of Demand: When price and total revenue change in the same direction, demand is inelastic; and when price and total revenue change in the opposite direction, demand is elastic.

APPLIED EXERCISES

EXERCISE 1:

Assume you are in the widget business and have the following demand schedule:

PRICE	QUANTITY
$10	10
$9	12
$8	13

What can you determine from the above information relative to price elasticity?

EXERCISE 2:

You have determined that the price elasticity of demand for your firm's product is 1.4 at the current price. If you are forced to increase your price by 10%, what is the expected change in quantity demanded? If you determined that the price elasticity was .6 instead, what would you expect would happen to quantity demanded?

EXERCISE 3:

Discuss the use of elasticity to set airline fares for individuals and for business travelers.

APPLIED EXERCISES: ANSWERS

EXERCISE 1:

The total revenue at $10 is $100; at $9 is $108, and at $8 is $104. Therefore, the quantity demanded is elastic between $10 and $9 because total revenue increases but inelastic between $9 and $8 because total revenue decreases at this point. The coefficient of elasticity between $10 and $9 is 1.7 and .7 between $9 and $8.

EXERCISE 2:

If the price elasticity of demand is 1.4 then a 10% increase in price will result in a 14% decrease in quantity demanded. If the price elasticity is .6, then a price increase of 10% will result in a 6% decrease in quantity demanded.

EXERCISE 3:

Prices for business travelers tend to be more inelastic than leisure travelers in part because business travelers have fewer substitute options.

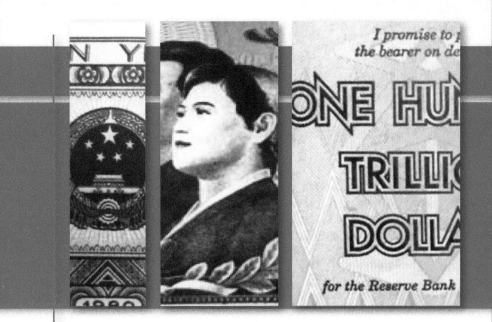

CONSUMER
BEHAVIOR

INTRODUCTION

Within capitalism, the consumer is the major determinant of what is produced. Lesson 5 discussed the sensitivity of consumers to changes in prices and in this lesson consumer decision making is considered.

LEARNING OBJECTIVES

Please note the listed objectives. As you will see, the course materials are all objective driven.
This provides you with a constant way to direct and monitor your progress throughout the course.

1 OBJECTIVE ONE

Describe utility.

2 OBJECTIVE TWO

Explain the concept of marginal utility and provide the correct interpretation for a related problem.

3 OBJECTIVE THREE

Explain the concept of consumer surplus and provide the correct interpretation for a related problem.

4 OBJECTIVE FOUR

Explain the equilibrium utility rule and provide the correct interpretation for a related problem.

5 OBJECTIVE FIVE

Describe the effect of time on consumer choices and its basis in the concept of utility.

1 INTERACTIVE EXERCISE

Explain the indifference curve model and provide the correct interpretation for a related problem.

Decisions describing consumer behavior

Consumer behavior metrics may appear at first to be complex but you as a consumer make decisions using this process intuitively. Economists have described this process methodically by quantifying the automatic analytical thinking of consumers.

For example, consider that you are given an extra $1,000 to spend. How do you decide what to buy? You currently know what purchases you would consider, but how do you make a decision? In economic terms, what combination of goods/services will maximize your total pleasure (utility)?

The History of Consumer Behavior Analysis

Consumer economics has been considered for over 150 years. In the early 1830s, Jeremy Bentham, a philosopher-economist, studied consumer behavior. Bentham concluded that consumers seek maximum utility (pleasure) with minimum cost expenditure.

Historically, economists have closely analyzed how consumers behave and why. The price/quantity demand line became the traditional representation of consumer behavior. Demand illustrates the inverse relationship between price and quantity because of three economic principles:

The income effect: According to the income effect, as the price declines for a good, it is as if you have more income and therefore you are more likely to buy a higher quantity.

Maximum utility (pleasure) with minimum cost expenditure

The substitution effect: According to the substitution effect, if the price of product x goes down, there will be an increase in quantity demanded for x from buyers of substitute goods due to a lower price.

The diminishing marginal utility effect According to microeconomic theory, as more of an item is consumed, the amount of additional satisfaction decreases and therefore, in order to sell more of a product, the vendor must reduce price to induce the consumer to buy more.

Traditional Supply and Demand Market Equilibrium

Price	Quantity Demanded	Quantity Supplied
$9.50	1	5
9.00	2	4
8.50	3	3
8.00	4	2
7.50	5	1

Let's again consider value from Lesson 4. The above demand and supply table illustrates consumer and producer behavior for a product. Consumers will buy more at a lower price and suppliers will supply more at a higher price, but the market is cleared by the equilibrium price of $8.50 where suppliers will bring three to the market and consumers will buy three.

CONSUMER SURPLUS

Notice that one person would have been willing to pay $9.50 and another would have been willing to pay $9.00 but if the price is in equilibrium at $8.50, where quantity demand equals quantity supplied, each consumer will only have to pay $8.50. The benefit received by paying a lower price than each consumer would have been willing to pay is consumer surplus.

Price	Quantity	Consumer Surplus
$10.00	0	0
9.50	1 (1 additional)	9.50 − 8.50 = 1.00
9.00	2 (1 additional)	9.00 − 8.50 = .50
	Total Consumer Surplus	= 1.50

ECONOMIC UTILITY

Economists measure the total utility and the marginal utility with changes in quantity of consumption. For example, assume you are consuming brownies with the following utility function.

Number of Brownies	Total Utility	Marginal Utility
0	0	
		10
1	10	
		8
2	18	
		5
3	23	
		0
4	23	

With the consumption of the first brownie, you received a total pleasure of 10 *utils* (units of utility). This is also an addition of 10 since you had a total of zero with zero units consumed. With the consumption of two units you gained a marginal utility of eight increasing total utility to 18. This process continues with a reduction in additional pleasure (marginal utility) with each additional unit consumed. There is an increase in total utility with each additional unit consumed until you reach four brownies consumed and at that point you gained no additional pleasure over the consumption of three. Notice that marginal utility values are actually positioned at the midpoint between changes in the units of brownies consumed. The amount of change (marginal utility) is represented as a movement from one unit to the next and is placed at the midpoint.

The marginal utility can be found from the total utility by subtracting the previous value. Total utility is 18 at two units consumed, then a value of 23 for three units consumed meaning that you had a marginal utility (additional utility) or increase of five. Given the total utility values, the marginal utility can be calculated, or given the marginal values the total can be calculated.

The Graphic Utility Function

Another **utility function** is shown in Table 6.1 and illustrated graphically in Figure 6.1. The total utility is the amount of total pleasure from consuming through a given quantity while the marginal utility is the amount of additional pleasure as one more unit is consumed.

TABLE 6.1

Quantity Consumed	Total Utility	Marginal Utility
0	0	
		50
1	50	
		90
2	140	
		80
3	220	
		65
4	285	
		45
5	330	
		5
6	335	
		5
7	340	
		-5
8	335	

The marginal utility line is illustrated on the same graph as total utility in Figure 6.1. The marginal utility cure will increase to the inflection of the total utility line. Marginal utility is zero where total utility is at a maximum. At the maximum of the total utility, the marginal utility is zero because total utility cannot be increased by consuming more units.

FIGURE 6.1

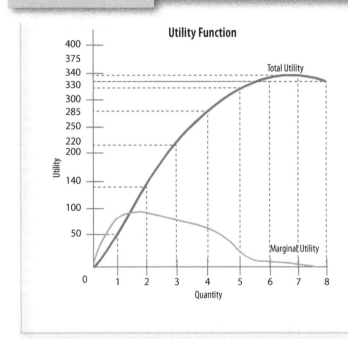

MARGINAL AND TOTAL UTILITY GRAPH

Notice in Figure 6.1 the total utility function values increase at an increasing rate (when marginal utility increases from 50 to 90) and then increase at a decreasing rate (when marginal utility decreases from 90 to 5) and then decrease (when marginal utility is a negative 5). When the eighth unit is consumed, displeasure is experienced and five units of total utility are actually lost.

The Law of Diminishing Returns

The law of diminishing returns states that as more units are consumed past some point of consumption, less additional pleasure will be received. The law of diminishing returns begins with the consumption of unit three.

As more units are consumed, there is a continual increase in utility from three through seven units but at a diminished marginal rate. The law of diminishing returns sets in with the consumption of unit three and continues throughout additional increases in consumption until negative returns are reached with the addition of unit eight. The maximum total pleasure is at seven units.

The Utility Maximization Rule

The utility maximization rule states that consumers should allocate their money income such that the last dollar spent on each product purchased yields the same amount of marginal satisfaction. The amount of pleasure per dollar is the marginal utility divided by the price for each item.

$$MUa/Pa = MUb/Pb = MUc/Pc$$

Utility Rule Application

Assume you are going to lunch and have a choice of two meals. The first meal would give an increase in marginal utility of 100 with a $25 price. The second meal would give you an increase of only 10 with a $2 price. Given only two options, which should you logically choose?

- MUa/Pa = MUb/Pb
  - if equilibrium exists (each is balanced)
  - 100/25 does not = 10/2 (no equilibrium present, therefore there is not an equal pleasure per dollar of each)
  - 100/25 = Four units of pleasure per dollar spent with $25 meal
  - 10/2 = Five units of pleasure per dollar spent with $2 meal

Therefore, logically you should select the $2 meal as this provides more additional utility per dollar spent (five units as opposed to four).

Finding Maximum Utility

To find the maximum pleasure combination of two choices, follow the steps below:

- Find the marginal utility as you purchase more of a given product (subtract total utility from previous consumption).
- Find the marginal utility per dollar of your additional consumption (divide marginal utility by price).
- Choose items with the most utility per dollar until all of your income is spent.

Illustrating Maximum Utility with Varied Consumption of Products R and S

These utility concepts can be applied to a decision to purchase given utility patterns for two goods as listed below. If you can buy good R and good S at a cost of $2 each, how many of each would you purchase if you have an income of $8 or $12?

TABLE 6.2

	CONSUMER EQUILIBRIUM		
Units of Good R	Total Utility of Good R	Units of Good S	Total Utility of Good S
1	10	1	14
2	18	2	26
3	24	3	36
4	28	4	44
5	30	5	50
6	30	6	54

To find the maximum total utility with a given income, one must find the marginal utility per dollar of each product for each additional unit consumed.

TABLE 6.3

Quantity	TUr	MUr	MU/Sr	TUs	MUs	MU/Ss
0	0			0		
		10	5		14	7
1	10			14		
		8	4		12	6
2	18			26		
		6	3		10	5
3	24			36		
		4	2		8	4
4	28			44		
		2	1		6	3
5	30			50		
		0	0		4	2
6	30			54		

Since the marginal utility per dollar is equal at five units of pleasure per dollar with the consumption of one unit of R and three units of S, the total cost would be (1 × $2) + (3 × $2) for a total cost of $8. The total amount of utility from this consumption would be 10 units from consumption of one unit of R and 36 units from consumption of three units of S, for a total utility of 46 units. Therefore with an income of $8, the maximum pleasure would occur consuming one unit of R and three units of S.

Reallocation Approach

Another method of finding maximum utility is to purchase each item with the highest marginal utility per dollar until all income is spent.

Using this method, how is an income of $12 best spent? First, one would buy one unit of S for seven units of pleasure per dollar(greater marginal utility per dollar than any other) for a cost of $2; then the next higher value is six at two units of S that would also cost $2. Thereby one has spent $4 for two units of S, but we would continue until all $12 is spent. The next purchase is at five units of pleasure per dollar at one additional unit of R and one additional unit of S. With three units of S and one unit of R we have spent $8. Next we would buy a total of two units of R and a total of four units of S for an additional pleasure per dollar of four units. Total cost of $12 is spent on two units of R (2 × $2 = $4) + and four units of S (4 × $2 = $8)—our maximum utility combination. The expenditure of $12 would yield a total pleasure of 18 units from R and 44 units from S for a total utility of 62 units.

Notice that as we spend more money our total pleasure increases to a maximum point but with additional increases in spending our marginal utility (additional pleasure) declines.

Utility and the Role of Savings

Savings (non-consumption) also has a utility function. Some individuals receive a higher utility from not spending then from consumption and thereby choose to save money.

UTILITY AND TIME

Time and opportunity cost are considered relative to utility. Questions regarding flying on vacation or driving may be based on the value of your time and the pleasure from driving or flying. The amount of pleasure is measured per dollar but also the opportunity cost of time lost from work must be included. Consider how this concept may explain why Americans may be wasteful of goods but protective of their leisure time.

The Ancient Comparison: Utility of Water and Diamonds

Traditional microeconomic theory of utility can be applied to the ancient paradox of the value of water versus diamonds. Which has greater utility: diamonds or water? Total utility applies to necessities such as water while marginal utility applies to your location on the total utility line. If you have the necessary amount of water, diamonds have greater immediate or marginal value. This value is not determined by supply and demand but rather by your utility function.

- Total Utility of Water > Total Utility of Diamonds however
- Marginal Utility of Diamonds > Marginal Utility of Water (given that you have sufficient water).

Budget Constraints

As consumers we are all limited by our income and therefore must limit our satisfaction to live within our budgets. The previous allocation approach, formulated as the utility maximization rule, set our purchases equal to the amount of additional pleasure per dollar and then applied the income constraint. Another approach to this process is to examine the combinations of products bought with a given increase in income and then find the amount of utility at that budget level.

Let's assume that we have $48 to spend on two goods, X and Y, and further assume that Product X costs $1.00 and Product Y costs $2.00. If we have an income of $48, what combination of goods will consume our income? Consider the table below featuring combinations of X and Y for possible purchases.

TABLE 6.4

Product X	Product Y	Expenditure
48	0	$48
40	4	48
32	8	48
24	12	48
0	24	48

FIGURE 6.2

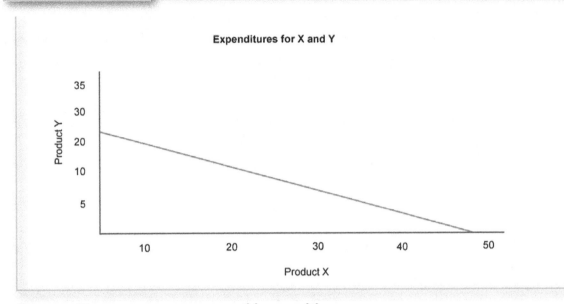

TOTAL EXPENDITURE FOR X AND Y

In Figure 6.2 the total budget constraint is illustrated using all of our income. The budget line constraint illustrates purchases that the consumer has with the total expenditure of funds. Any combination outside of this consumption possibilities curve is unattainable and any combination inside would not consume our total income.

THE INDIFFERENCE CURVE

We now need to know the combinations of X and Y that will yield the same utility, called an indifference curve. The indifference curve is the combination of goods/services that will result in the same amount of satisfaction with constant income and prices. The table below assumes equal amounts of pleasure with varied purchases of X and Y.

Product X	Product Y
50	4
40	6
32	8
27	10

When graphed, the indifference curve is curved rather than a straight line (linear) because of the principle of diminishing marginal utility. As an individual consumes more of a product, the marginal utility declines and therefore up to a point one will substitute X for Y. The change in X to Y is the marginal rate of substitution. Finally, however, a point of consumption is reached with a decreasing rate of substitution and the indifference function becomes flat.

FIGURE 6.3

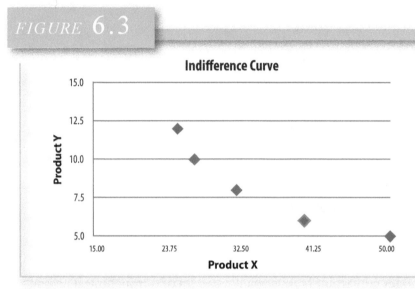

TOTAL EXPENDITURES FOR X AND Y

TABLE 6.5

EXPENDITURES FOR X AND Y		
Product X	Product Y	Expenditure
48	0	$48
40	4	48
32	8	48
24	12	48
0	24	48

TABLE 6.6

INDIFFERENCE FOR X AND Y	
Product X	Product Y
50	4
40	4
32	8
27	10

By combining the budget constraint line with the indifference curve, the maximum utility position is found to be where $32 is spent on X and $16 on Y. One can find these locations on both the expenditures model and the indifference model. Therefore, one can conclude the maximum utility position is $32 of X and $16 of Y, the point of tangency for the budget constraint line and the indifference curve.

Graphically Representing Indifference Utility

Consider Figure 6.4 to describe the maximum utility value graphically.

FIGURE 6.4

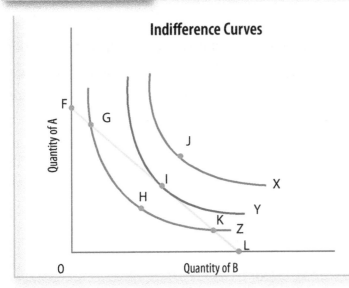

Indifference Curves

GRAPHIC INDIFFERENCE CURVE

The curved lines X, Y, and Z represent the combination for consumption of product A and product B that will yield the same amount of additional pleasure. Along given lines of X, Y, and Z, the consumer is indifferent to the consumption (yielding the same about of total satisfaction). The straight line F L represents a budget line or the amount of funds available for consumption. The intercept of Y curve with budget line F L (at I) is the combination of A and B that will yield the maximum level of satisfaction. The higher the indifference curve, the higher the amount of total satisfaction. Therefore, position J has higher satisfaction than position I, and I has higher satisfaction than H.

Critics of Utility Theory

One of the most noted critics of utility theory was the American economist Thorstein Veblen. Veblen described utility values of the 20th century as different from consumption of earlier times. His concept of conspicuous consumption suggested that the amount of pleasure attained by individuals is subjective and social in nature, concluding that utility is difficult to analyze.

Economists recognize the difficulty in measuring pleasure directly, but analysis is possible by comparing marginal values between products. The marginal utility per dollar compared to other purchases is an important concept for brand comparisons among goods and services.

In Conclusion

An understanding of consumer behavior is an important part of comprehending the allocation of resources by individuals. Consumption decisions are made based upon a logical process valuing utility, price, and income alternatives. Firms seek to understand this process in order to better serve consumers. Firms employ brand managers to allocate resources to effectively serve consumers on a product or service. These decisions might involve redesigning products or better targeting consumer markets with information.

REAL WORLD ECONOMICS

How is utility for goods/services measured in the real world of economics?

The most recognized measure of utility value associated with consumption of goods and services is customer satisfaction. The American Customer Satisfaction Index (ACSI) has measured comparable customer satisfaction among 200 companies in 43 industries since 1994.

The ACSI is calculated by the University of Michigan in Ann Arbor, Michigan. The Index consists of interviews with 80,000 consumers input into an econometric model. The published Index is available annually at the end of the year.

This Index is highly respected and firms are sensitive to the measure of utility for their products/services. The Index is also closely monitored by all sectors of the economy.

Who are the "Winners?"

Current firms with the highest index values include: Lexus, BMW, Toyota, Honda, Apple, and Google. The ACSI is available through the Web.

Consumer Behavior Theory is an explanation of how consumers react to changes in price as described by the price and quantity demanded.

Consumer Equilibrium—Utility Maximization Rule: A consumer should allocate additional income such that the amount of additional pleasure per dollar is equal for all additional purchases.

Consumer Surplus is the amount consumers save by buying at the equilibrium price rather than a higher price they would have been willing to pay.

Law of Diminishing Marginal Utility is an economic principle that states as more units are consumed, a point will be reached that results in less additional satisfaction with the consumption of more units.

Marginal Utility is the amount of additional pleasure received with an increase in the consumption of a good.

Utility is the amount of pleasure received with the consumption of a good or service.

Utility and Indifference Analysis: An indifference curve illustrates different amounts of consumption of two items that yield the same amount of satisfaction.

EXERCISE 1 :

Considering the following marginal utilities and prices with a budget = $20, how much would you purchase of each? Assume A costs $2 each and B costs $1 each. How much total utility will be received for $20?

QUANTITY	MARGINAL UTILITY A	MARGINAL UTILITY B
1	50	30
2	44	28
3	38	26
4	32	24
5	26	22
6	20	20
7	12	16
8	4	10

APPLIED EXERCISES

EXERCISE 2:

Complete the blank spaces in the following utility table for consumption of pieces of candy.

Q OF CANDY	TOTAL UTILITY	MARGINAL UTILITY
1	?	20
2	35	?
3	?	10
4	50	?

EXERCISE 3:

Assume that the marginal utilities for the first three units of a good consumed are 200, 150, and 125, respectively. What is the total utility of three units? Is this illustrative of the law of diminishing marginal utility?

EXERCISE 4:

John Brown gains 180 units of marginal utility from buying an additional pair of slacks and 100 units of marginal utility from buying an additional tie. Slacks cost $120 and ties cost $100. Which should he purchase?

APPLIED EXERCISES: ANSWERS

EXERCISE 1:

	MUA	MUA/PA	MUB	MUB/PB
1	50	25	30	30
2	44	22	28	28
3	38	19	26	26
4	32	16	24	24
5	26	13	22	22
6	20	10	20	20
7	12	6	16	16
8	4	2	10	10

Notice that the MUA/PA = MUB/PB at 2 of A and 5 of B; also at 4 of A and 7 of B; and at 6 of A and 8 of B. Since the budget is $20, this expenditure is at equilibrium at 6 of A and 8 of B where 6 times $2 = $12 for A and 8 times $1 = $8 for B taken together = $12 + $8 for a total of $20. Total utility for 6 units of A will be the MUA for units 1-6 consumed: 50 + 44 + 38 + 32 + 26 + 20 = 210 and for total utility of B will be the MUB for units 1-10 consumed: 30 + 28 + 26 + 24 + 22 + 20 + 16 + 10 = 176 for a total utility of 210 + 176 = 386.

APPLIED EXERCISES: ANSWERS

EXERCISE 2 :

Q of Candy	Total Utility	Marginal Utility
1	20	20
2	35	15
3	45	10
4	50	5

EXERCISE 3 :

Total utility is: 200 + 150 + 125 = 475 and because the marginal increases are declining, this does illustrate the law of diminishing marginal utility.

EXERCISE 4 :

Slacks: 180/120 = 1.5 marginal utility value for Slacks. Ties: 100/100 = 1.0 marginal utility value for ties. Therefore John should purchase the slacks.

INTRODUCTION

Our study now combines what we have learned about price from Lesson 5 with utility theory from Lesson 6 to allocate resources among cost factors. Consider that you own a firm that understands consumer satisfaction and consumer reaction to price changes, but now you must also make cost/output decisions. This process is production analysis.

LEARNING OBJECTIVES

Please note the listed objectives. As you will see, the course materials are all objective driven. This provides you with a constant way to direct and monitor your progress throughout the course.

1 OBJECTIVE ONE

Define: opportunity cost, economic cost, implicit cost, and explicit cost. Give an example for each.

2 OBJECTIVE TWO

Distinguish between normal profit, economic profit, and accounting profit. Also distinguish between the terms short run and long run.

3 OBJECTIVE THREE

Describe the production function model and provide the correct interpretation for a related problem.

4 OBJECTIVE FOUR

Explain the various costs of the short-run costs of production model and provide a correct interpretation for a related problem.

5 OBJECTIVE FIVE

Describe the long-run cost production model and provide the correct interpretation for a related problem.

1 INTERACTIVE EXERCISE

Distinguish between the law of diminishing returns and the concepts of economies and diseconomies of scale.

Economic views of firm cost

Economists value resource allocation relative to other alternatives. Costs are defined specifically within economics by the following classifications;

Opportunity cost is the actual economic cost to accomplish something. This is the cost of the next best alternative that had to be sacrificed (given up) to acquire a given activity.

Economics costs are the total sacrifice that must be made to do something or acquire something. For example, the cost of taking this course is not just the text, tuition, and transportation, but also the time you must sacrifice for study when you could have been working. The economic cost of the course might include: text, $100; tuition, $500; transportation, $700; and lost wages (70 hours at $12 hour) $840 for a total of $2,140.

A **firm's economic cost** is that payment a firm must make in order to attract resources from alternative production (alternative costs) and maintain the operation. Assume you are starting a new business that requires an investment of $100,000 but you could have invested in another endeavor for the same amount with the same risk and received a 20% return. You have sacrificed a $20,000 return and this is an opportunity cost of using the funds for your business. You must not only cover all costs for production but you must also cover your own opportunity cost as well.

Explicit and Implicit Costs

Explicit costs are payments to outsiders or non-owners. Explicit costs are also called accounting costs. Most costs of operating a business are explicit costs such as payments to workers, suppliers of materials, and building or equipment costs.

Implicit costs are payments to self-employed resources and are non-cash costs or alternative costs. Profit is often the largest implicit cost. In economics, a firm must make a "normal profit" to continue the business since owner resources could have received a return from alternative uses. This normal profit (return) is an expected cost (implicit cost) of doing business.

Maximum utility (pleasure) with minimum cost expenditure

The Economic Cost Equation

Economic Costs = Explicit Costs + Implicit Costs

AN ECONOMIC APPLICATION

Assume you invested $100,000 into your lawn-mowing business but you could have invested in a similar operation with the same risk and received a 20 percent return. If your explicit costs (payments to workers, equipment, etc.) are $60,000 and your total revenue is $120,000, then your economic profit is $40,000. $120,000 total revenue minus $60,000 (explicit costs) minus $20,000 (normal profit that you could have received from another investment, alternative costs) = $40,000 economic profit.

Normal profit is a minimum payment needed to sustain the enterprise. This is the alternative cost or what is reasonable and necessary as a return. An economic profit is a profit after all economic costs including a normal profit are deducted from total revenue.

Economic Profit = Total Revenue − Total Economic Cost

Economic Costs = Implicit + Explicit Costs

Accounting Profit = Total Revenue − Explicit Costs

Accountants do not consider a normal profit as a cost, therefore their formula for net profit (accounting profit) is total revenue minus payments to non-owners (explicit costs).

Economic Time Variables

Economists consider costs in two time frames: short run and long run. The short run is a time period too brief to increase capacity but a sufficient time to increase operations to maximum capacity (output). The short run considers the intensity of use with a fixed plant size.

For example, assume you have a widget manufacturing plant, in the short run you would be able to increase to the maximum production but you could not increase the size of the plant. You could increase operating hours and make full use of resources to maximum capacity operating 24 hours per day, seven days per week.

The **long run** is a time period long enough to change all inputs (land, labor, capital, and ownership) and therefore change capacity. In the long run you could build a larger plant or purchase an existing operation to combine with your own firm.

> **LONG-RUN:**
>
> A time period long enough to change all inputs thereby changing capacity

THE ECONOMIC OUTPUT/COST VARIABLES: THE PRODUCTION FUNCTION

Economists compare varied costs relative to output. The production function is inputs (such as units of labor) compared to outputs (quantity produced).

The **total product** (TP) is the quantity of output and is graphed on the y-axis while the number of inputs is graphed on the x-axis. Consider Figure 7.1. We have used this data previously for utility and will now apply the same data to production for simplicity of calculation. Notice the relationship of total product and marginal product is the same as the utility function.

TABLE 7.1

Number of Workers	Total Product	Marginal Production
0	0	
1	50	50
2	140	90
3	200	60
4	285	85
5	330	45
6	335	5
7	340	5
8	335	−5

FIGURE 7.1

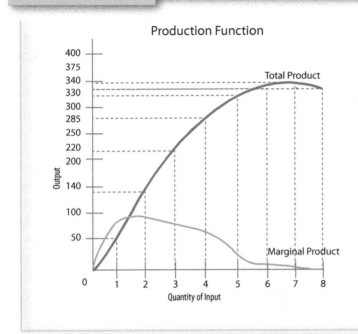

GRAPH OF TOTAL PRODUCT CURVE AND MARGINAL PRODUCT.

Marginal Product

The marginal product (MP) is the change in total product from a change in input resources. Marginal product is the additional output with one additional worker or the loss of output with one fewer worker.

Marginal Product = The change in output (number of "widgets")
divided by the change in input (labor).

Notice in Figure 7.1 that the total product of labor curve increases at an increasing rate (units 1-2), then increases at a decreasing rate (units 3-7) and finally decreases after the eighth unit of labor is added. The TP curve is at a maximum at 7 units of input because the MP equals zero at this point (contributes no increase in output with more input).

The Production Function Matrix Applied

Let's apply our understanding to one more application:

Number of Workers/Laborers	Output Total Product	Additional Output Marginal Product
0	0	
		10
1	10	
		15
2	25	
		20
3	45	
		15
4	60	
		10
5	70	
		5
6	75	
		2
7	77	
		1
8	78	
		-1
9	77	
		-2
10	75	

There are many factors involved in deciding on how many workers to employ, but several observations can be made using economic reasoning. Notice that at two workers, the marginal product is at a maximum. We would consider employing more workers as long as the marginal product value is increasing in line with marginal costs; however, when the marginal product is decreasing (as after two workers) because labor is expensive, we may decide to produce with only two workers depending upon quantity demanded and price.

Given the above production function, we would not employ worker #9 or #10 as their work actually reduces total output.

Other Economic Cost Measures

Economists measure costs with several metrics to find the most effective use of resources. **Fixed costs** are costs that remain the same (constant) regardless of output. There are many fixed costs in running a business including property taxes, insurance, and depreciation.

As an example of these costs, assume we operate a pepper food plant as an agri-business. The operation of the pepper plant would encounter both fixed and variable costs. Fixed costs include land, renting equipment, property taxes, insurance, a toll-free phone, and depreciation.

Variable costs are costs that vary directly with the amount of output. When a manufacturer increases output, there will be increased costs with output for variables such as labor, materials, and shipping costs. As more units are produced, the total variable costs increase. Variable costs at a pepper food plant would include water, plants, fertilizer, and labor.

Average costs: Economists also analyze the average costs (costs per unit of output). By finding the total cost and dividing by the number of units produced, average or per-unit costs are found.

AVERAGE COSTS

Average Total Cost (ATC) = Total Cost (TC) / Quantity Produced (Q)

Average Variable Cost (AVC) = Total Variable Cost (TVC) / Quantity (Q)

Average Fixed Cost (AFC) = Total Fixed Cost (TFC) / Quantity (Q)

Average Total Cost (ATC) = Average Variable Cost + Average Fixed Cost
      (ATC)   (AVC)   (AFC)

TOTAL COST COMBINATIONS

Total Costs (TC) = Total Variable Cost (TVC) + Total Fixed Cost (TFC)

Total Costs (TC) = Average Total Cost (ATC) x Quantity (Q)

MARGINAL COST

Marginal cost is a critical variable in microeconomics. Marginal cost (MC) is the additional cost of producing one more unit of output. Comparisons of marginal cost with marginal revenue (amount of additional revenue per unit) are essential in finding maximum profit output in microeconomics.

$$MC = \frac{\text{Chage in TC}}{\text{Change in Quantity}}$$

Economic Cost Practice Exercise

Using the following total cost (TC) related to output (quantity produced), complete the table of values using appropriate formulas. The answers follow in Table 7.3.

TABLE 7.2

Output	TFC	+ TVC =	TC	AFC	AVC	ATC	MC
0	___	___	110	___	___	___	
1	___	___	170	___	___	___	___
2	___	___	220	___	___	___	___
3	___	___	260	___	___	___	___
4	___	___	320	___	___	___	___
5	___	___	420	___	___	___	___
6	___	___	560	___	___	___	___
7	___	___	740	___	___	___	___
8	___	___	960	___	___	___	___
9	___	___	1220	___	___	___	___
10	___	___	1520	___	___	___	___

TABLE 7.3

Output	TFC	+ TVC	= TC	AFC	AVC	ATC	MC
0	110	0	110		0		
							60
1	110	60	170	110	60	170	
							50
2	110	110	220	55	55	110	
							40
3	110	150	260	36.7	50	86.7	
							60
4	110	210	320	27.5	52.5	80	
							100
5	110	310	420	22	62	84	
							140
6	110	450	560	18.3	75	93.3	
							180
7	110	630	740	15.7	90	105.7	
							220
8	110	850	960	13.8	106.3	120	
							260
9	110	1110	1220	12.2	123.3	135.5	
							300
10	110	1410	1520	11	141	152	

TABLE 7.4

COST OF PRODUCING BROWNIES	
Quantity of Brownies	Total Cost
0	2.50
1	2.60
2	2.68
3	2.75
4	2.80
5	2.85
6	2.96
7	4.20
8	6.80

Let's now apply our costs in a different form to a firm called Brownies United.

Using the above cost data for producing brownies, economic cost relationships can be calculated.

The **total fixed cost** is the cost of not producing (quantity = 0). The total fixed cost (FC) above is $2.50 because the cost at no output is $2.50.

The **totoal average total cost** is the total cost divided by quantity. The average cost (ATC) of producing 4 brownies is $2.80 /4 = $.70 (per unit).

The **total variable cost (VC)** is the total cost minus fixed cost. The total cost of 4 brownies is $2.80 less the fixed cost of $2.50 = the total variable cost $.30.

The **average variable cost (AVC)** at 4 units is the total variable cost divided by 4 or $.30/4 = $.075.

The **average fixed cost (AFC)** is the fixed cost divided by quantity. Fixed cost = $2.50 and average fixed cost at 4 units = $2.50/4 = $.625.

Average fixed cost + average variable cost = average total cost or $.625 + .075 = $.70, or total cost of 4 is $2.80 divided by quantity = $.70.

The average fixed cost (AFC) is a decreasing value with increasing output because AFC is the same value divided by a larger quantity.

In the above brownie production, the marginal cost of increasing output from 4 units to 5 units is the total cost at 4 units minus the total cost of producing 5 units.

Total cost of quantity = 5 is $2.85 and the total cost of quantity = 4 is $2.80, therefore the marginal cost of the fifth unit is $.05.

The Law of Diminishing Returns

The law of diminishing returns is the basic principle that as more is produced, eventually less additional output will result with each input. Marginal product (MP) is the amount of additional product produced by one additional worker. When there is less additional output added by each additional worker (MP), the MC will increase. MC is a U-shaped curve when graphed with output on the y-axis and input on the x-axis due to the economic principle of the law of diminishing returns.

As more workers are hired, the marginal product may increase at first but after some amount of additional input, less marginal product (additional output) will be produced. If MC is increasing, marginal product (MP) is decreasing and if MC is decreasing, the MP must be increasing.

The Marginal Cost Intercept

The marginal cost (MC) curve, the average total cost (ATC) curve and average variable cost (AVC) curve have an important economic relationship.

- When the ATC or AVC is increasing, then the marginal curves are above it. Consider this relationship with test scores; if your average is going up, it is because the marginal (last score) is above the average.

- When ATC or AVC is decreasing, then the marginal curve is below the average.

- When the average curve is neither increasing nor decreasing, then the result is a minimum value. The MC curve intersects the ATC and the AVC at their minimum points. The lowest points on the AVC or ATC curves are at the intersections with the MC curve.

MC = ATC at the minimum of ATC

MC = AVC at the minimum of AVC

FIGURE 7.2

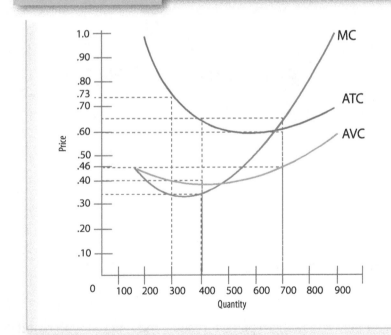

Notice in Figure 7.2 that the minimum of the ATC and the AVC curves are at the intercept with MC.

Further notice the difference between the ATC and the AVC is the AFC (ATC = AVC + AFC).

GRAPH OF MC, ATC AND AVC

The Marginal Product Concept

A reasoned relationship also exists with total product (TP) and marginal product (MP).

- If the total product (TP) is increasing at an increasing rate, then the marginal product (MP) is increasing.

- If the total product (TP) is increasing at a decreasing rate, then the marginal product (MP) is decreasing but remains positive. As long as the MP is positive, the TP will be increasing.

- If the total product (TP) is not increasing (change of zero) the rate MP = 0, the TP is at a maximum.

TIME/COST RELATIONSHIP FOR A FIRM

Output choices in the production process are determined by changes in cost with changes in output. The short-run (assumes a fixed capacity) average cost (SRAC) curve is U-shaped because of the law of diminishing returns. As more inputs (workers) are added with a fixed capacity, past some point, the average cost per unit will increase because the MP is decreasing.

FIGURE 7.3

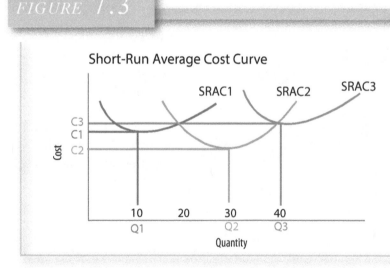

SHORT-RUN AVERAGE COST CURVES

Figure 7.3 depicts three different plant capacities (plant 1, plant 2 and plant 3) with resulting variances in short-run average cost (SRAC) curves. Plant one (shown in violet) has the SRAC1 that has a U-shaped curve with low quantities of output capacity. The SRAC1 is at a minimum average cost at C1/Q1. In order to increase output, a new plant is built (plant 2 in light violet) resulting in a decreased average cost of output when producing more than 20 units to 40 units (SRAC2). SRAC2 is at a minimum average cost at C2/Q2. SRAC2 is the lowest average cost for most output quantities. When a larger capacity is built (plant 3 in green) represented by SRAC3, the minimum average cost is C3/Q3, representing an increase in average costs from SRAC2.

Plant 2 has lower costs with increasing output compared to plant 1 due to **economies of scale** while plant 3 has higher costs than plant 2 due to **diseconomies of scale.** Economies of scale cause average costs to decline with increases in capacity due to efficiency of production. Diseconomies of scale cause average costs to increase with increases in capacity due to production inefficiencies.

Notice at a quantity of more than 20 but less than 40 units of output, plant 2 has lower average total costs than plant 1. Plant 2 is the minimum cost output for quantities of more than 20 but less than 40 units. Costs go down from plant 1 to plant 2 because of economies of scale associated with increased output.

Economies of Scale

Economies of scale reduce average total costs (costs per unit) because of:

- Increased specialization of labor. As more workers are added to a production operation, each worker is able to specialize and often increase his/her productivity (output per worker hour).
- Increased productivity of management. As a firm adds workers, the span of control for each manager (number of workers per manager) is able to increase with greater resulting efficiency. When the operation is small, one manager may supervise only 2 employees but with a large firm, a supervisor may be able to manage 5 to 10 workers.
- Increased use of capital resources. Computerized or automated systems decrease costs with increases in output. Within a larger organization, more funds are available to purchase more capital goods such as with automated manufacturing.

THE ECONOMIC LONG RUN

In the long run a firm has no fixed capacity. The firm can select any size of plant capacity. The long-run average total cost curve (LRATC) is called the planning curve because producers can plan in the long run which plant is the best size to maximize profits.

The long-run average total cost (LRATC) curve is U-shaped because of economies and diseconomies of scale. As production is increased with increased plant sizes, the minimum average cost with each larger-sized plant will have decreasing costs but finally increasing costs per unit. In the example in Figure 7.3, there are three plant sizes with three different short-run average cost curves, SRAC1, SRAC2, and SRAC3. As production is moved from SRAC1 to SRAC2, the average costs go down but notice as production is increased from SRAC2 to SRAC3, the average costs increase. The decreasing costs with increasing plant capacity are called economies of scale (SRAC1 to SRAC2). The increasing costs with increasing plant capacity are called diseconomies of scale (SRAC2 to SRAC3).

The Long-Run Planning Curve

The long-run average total cost curve (LRATC) is U-shaped and tangent to the SRATC curves at their minimum points. This planning curve is the most efficient level of output for a given size of plant.

FIGURE 7.4

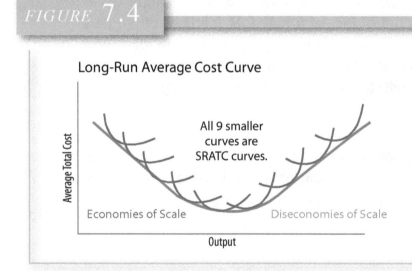

LONG-RUN AVERAGE COST CURVES FORM LONG-RUN PLANNING CURVE

DISECONOMIES OF SCALE

Over the higher levels of output, the LRATC curve values do increase after a minimum point is reached through economies of scale and then diseconomies of scale encountered. Increasing LRATC is experienced when with each increase in plant size, average costs increase.

Diseconomies of scale are considered to be due to managerial problems associated with operating a large organization. As output increases beyond some point, average costs begin to increase. Controlling costs in a large operation is often more difficult than in a small operation.

The Incidence of Economies and Diseconomies of Scale

Methods of dealing with diseconomies of scale involve techniques of management principles. Industries throughout the world have studied how workers can best maximize their labor input. The conclusions are widely varied but most theories suggest that greater involvement of the workers increases output. Matching authority with responsibility is an essential dimension of the management paradigm for both individuals and firms. The nature of human behavior and efficient production operations are closely integrated. Labor costs are generally the highest resource cost of a business and therefore high labor productivity is essential.

The shape of the LRATC curve is consistent among industries, but the framework of when economies and diseconomies begin relative to output does vary between industries. Some industries are known as having extensive economies of scale. In these industries, the planning curve has economies of scale throughout most plant sizes (LRATC1 in Figure 7.5). Industries with extensive economies of scale will often have high fixed costs and therefore, increasing output will allow absorption of costs over greater output. The automobile, steel, and computer chip industries are typical of this relationship.

Another type of cost relationship exists in firms with initial economies of scale but then diseconomies are encountered at relatively small output levels (LRATC2 shown in Figure 7.5). This type of firm is characterized by advantages of an on-site manager/owner in control of costs such as in a small retail shop. Specialty stores from card shops to hair salons often require on-site

Labor costs are generally the highest resource cost

owner involvement with customers and workers to be successful; therefore large scale operations encounter increasing costs at lower levels of output than found in LRATC1.

FIGURE 7.5

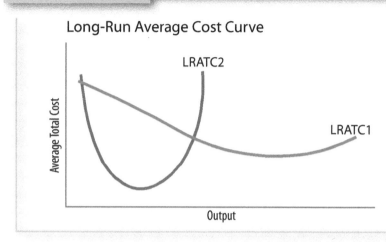

Long-Run Average Cost Curve

LRATC2

LRATC1

Average Total Cost

Output

LONG-RUN AVERAGE COST CURVE WITH VARIED INDUSTRY

Conclusion

Understanding the relationships of cost to output is essential to operating a firm successfully. The analysis of the operating relationships is a basic principle of microeconomics. Every firm must allocate considering output to costs in both the short run and the long run. Economies and diseconomies of scale must be considered relative to marginal factors of supply to minimize costs relative to revenue. Unit three will discuss the four market models that determine cost and revenue relationships.

FIGURE 7.6

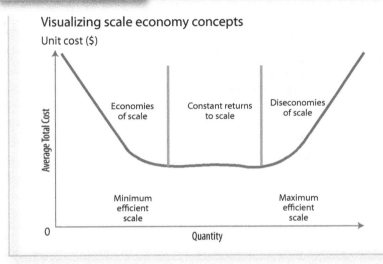

Visualizing scale economy concepts

Source: USDA, ERS.

REAL WORLD ECONOMICS

HOW REAL ARE ECONOMIES OF SCALE IN TODAY'S FIRMS?

The US Department of Agriculture has documented applications of economies of scale in corn, hog, and dairy production. These studies were from varied areas of the United States over a period of many years. Although factors other than scale of operation do influence costs, the operational cost is dominated by scale of operation.

According to USDA Research Service, corn produced in 1996 showed economies with costs under $2.50 per bushel for 85% of output. Farms producing at costs above this range were at a disadvantage. According to a 2004 study, hog the farmers with the lowest cost were from large, geographically concentrated areas where farmers' main occupation was solely farming. A number of characteristics are common to large scale output: close to market, fertile land, operated by farmers with technical knowledge for scale production.

A study of dairy farmers had similar conclusions and graphically displayed economic characteristics from Lesson 7. Farmers operating in the lowest zone of costs are in the minimum efficient scale area while those having diseconomies of scale are likely to be forced out of business in the long run.

Diseconomies of Scale is an increase in average costs attributed to increases in output associated with problems of managing large-scale firms.

Economic Cost is a cost of maintaining a business including a normal profit.

Economic Profit/Economic Loss: Profits greater than normal profit and losses are less than normal profit. Computed as Total Revenue minus Total Economic Costs = Economic Profit > 0; Economic Costs < 0

Economies of Scale is a decrease in average costs attributed to increases in output such as better use of management or efficiency through automation.

Explicit Costs are payments made to outsiders (non-owners) of the firm.

Fixed Costs are costs that remain constant regardless of output quantity.

Implicit Costs are costs paid to self-employed resources within the firm.

Law of Diminishing Returns is a principle where decreases in marginal output are associated with increases in input.

Long Run is the time period where all variables to a firm are variable in the long run including capacity.

Marginal Cost is the additional cost of one more unit found by dividing changes in total cost by the change in output.

Normal Profit is the amount of profit necessary to maintain the operation of the firm.

Opportunity Cost is the cost of the next best alternative that had to be sacrificed for a given opportunity.

Short Run is the time period allowing an increase to capacity but cannot change capacity.

Total Costs are all economic costs including both explicit and implicit costs.

Total Product/Marginal Product: Total product is the total output with a given input; marginal product is additional output with a given input.

Variable Costs are costs directly associated with increases in output, calculated by subtracting fixed costs from total cost.

APPLIED EXERCISES:

EXERCISE 1 :

Complete the marginal product in the table of the production function and note where the law of diminishing returns begins.

NUMBER OF WORKERS LABORERS	OUTPUT TOTAL PRODUCT	ADDITIONAL OUTPUT MARGINAL PRODUCT
1	10	
2	25	
3	45	
4	60	
5	70	
6	75	
7	77	
8	78	
9	77	
10	75	

APPLIED EXERCISES

EXERCISE 2 :

Complete the cost table below.

Q	TFC	TVC	TC	AFC	AVC	ATC	MC
0	——	——	$25	——	——	——	——
1	——	——	27	——	——	——	——
2	——	——	30	——	——	——	——
3	——	——	34	——	——	——	——
4	——	——	39	——	——	——	——
5	——	——	45	——	——	——	——
6	——	——	52	——	——	——	——
7	——	——	62	——	——	——	——
8	——	——	82	——	——	——	——
9	——	——	103	——	——	——	——
10	——	——	125	——	——	——	——

EXERCISE 1 :

NUMBER OF WORKERS LABORERS	OUTPUT TOTAL PRODUCT	ADDITIONAL OUTPUT MARGINAL PRODUCT
1	10	10
2	25	15
3	45	20
4	60	15
5	70	10
6	75	5
7	77	2
8	78	1
9	77	−1
10	75	−2

The law of diminishing returns begins with the addition of the fourth worker as the marginal product decreases from 20 to 15.

APPLIED EXERCISES: ANSWERS

EXERCISE 2 :

Q	TFC	TVC	TC	AFC	AVC	ATC	MC
0	25		$25				
1	25	2	27	25	2	27	2
2	25	5	30	12.5	2.5	15	3
3	25	9	34	8.3	3	11.3	4
4	25	14	39	6.3	3.5	9.8	5
5	25	20	45	5	4	9	6
6	25	27	52	4.2	4.5	8.7	7
7	25	37	62	3.6	5.3	8.9	10
8	25	57	82	3.1	7.2	10.3	20
9	25	78	103	2.7	8.7	11.4	21
10	25	100	125	2.5	10	12.5	22

Lesson 8

PURE
COMPETITION

INTRODUCTION

Unit 3 applies the principles of previous units to business operations in different market models. Firms are significantly influenced by their market environment.

LEARNING OBJECTIVES

Please note the listed objectives. As you will see, the course materials are all objective driven. This provides you with a constant way to direct and monitor your progress throughout the course.

1 OBJECTIVE ONE

Describe the four market models that are used to evaluate individual business and specific industries.

2 OBJECTIVE TWO

Demonstrate an understanding of the pure competition model and describe its economic characteristics.

3 OBJECTIVE THREE

Explain the cost and revenue relationships that exist for a business in a pure competition environment.

4 OBJECTIVE FOUR

Determine the optimum level of output for a business using a table of cost and revenue information (TR/ TC approach and MR/MC approach).

5 OBJECTIVE FIVE

Determine the optimum level of output for a business using a graph of cost and revenue information (TR/ TC approach and MR/MC approach).

I INTERACTIVE EXERCISE

Explain the advantages (benefits) and disadvantages (costs, risks) that are in a pure competition model and its evolution into the long-run.

Introduction to Market Models

There are four types of market models within capitalism, each with varied cost and revenue relationships. In each market model, economic conditions strongly influence resource allocation.

Pure competition, the most competitive and efficient market model, is presented in this Lesson. Pure competition is exemplified by individual farmers in agriculture. Monopoly is analyzed in Lesson 9, representing the least competition, like many utilities. Lesson 10 examines monopolistically competitive models, like a retail store and oligopoly models, like an airline firm.

OVERVIEW OF FOUR MARKET MODELS

Each of the four market models possesses varied economic characteristics. The central economic operations of the firm revolve around these comparable economic differences. The table below contrasts the major economic mechanisms among models.

TABLE 8.1

Market Model	Number of Producers	Product Differences	Control Over Price	Marketing Methods	Industry Example
Pure Competition	Large Number	Identical Products	None	Market Exchange	Argriculture
Monopolistic competition	Many	Differentiated	Some	Advertising	Retail
Oligopoly	Few	Identical or Differentiated	Some	Advertising	Steel, Oil, Airlines
Monopoly	One	No Substitues	Considerable	Public Relations	Some Utilities/ Drug Firms

Overview of four market models

A market structure with maximum competition

- Large number of producers.
- Identical products.
- No control over price by producers.
- Price is set by market.
- Example: agriculture industry.

A market structure where sellers produce similar, but slightly differentiated products

- Many producers.
- Differentiated products.
- Some control over price.
- Marketing through advertising
- Example: Retail

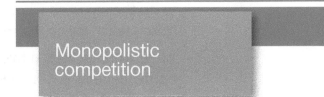

A market condition with only a few large sellers

- A few producers.
- Identical or differentiated products.
- Some control over price.
- Marketing through advertising.
- Example: Steel, oil, and airlines.

A market structure with no competition

- One producer.
- No substitute product.
- Considerable control over price.
- Marketing by public relations.
- Examples: Utilities, drug firms.

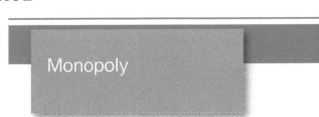

Pure competition as a market model

Pure competition is a unique market structure providing output at the lowest cost over the long run.

Pure competition is described by the following economic characteristics:

- A large number of buyers and sellers in the market, none of whom can individually affect the price of the product or service being bought or sold.

- A homogenous (standardized) product or service offered in an open market where products are perfectly substitutable. An individual farmer operates in this market and his product is assumed to be the same as all other farmers' products. The producer is a "price taker" since the market sets the price.

- Buyers and sellers in this market act to maximize their own economic benefit. Buyers will purchase at the lowest price and sellers will sell at the highest price.

- The market is open to new suppliers with easy entry and easy exit of producers. Any producer can enter such a market and any producer can exit as well.

Pure Competition and Perfect Competition

The purely competitive model is sometimes contrasted with the theoretical maximum of competition called perfect competition. Perfect competition assumes perfect market information (everyone in the market knows the price of the good or service) and perfect mobility of goods/services (all goods and services can be delivered anywhere in the world).

> Maximum Utility (pleasure) with minimum cost expeniture

Examples of Pure Competition

Pure competition is the benchmark of efficiency, but there are few examples of such competition. A widely held stock on the New York Stock Exchange and individual farmers are frequently cited as modeling pure competition.

However, farming has government subsidizes and the NYSE is regulated by government. This is inconsistent with a truly purely competitive market. In theory, pure competition is self-regulating without government assistance or regulation.

Why Study Pure Competition?

Each of the four market models possesses varied economic characteristics. The central economic operations of the firm revolve around these comparable economic differences. Table 8.1 contrasts the major economic mechanisms among models

Pure competition is important to economists because:

- Pure competition is the "finest hour" of capitalism with the lowest prices and the most responsiveness to consumers.

- Pure competition has few components so it is easy to understand graphically and mathematically (cost and revenue relationships are relatively simple).

- Pure competition is the "standard" of comparison to measure for productive and allocative efficiency.

The Purely Competitive Industry and the Individual Firm

The industry demand curve is the combination of demand curves of a large number of individual buyers with no single buyer influencing the resulting demand (price/quantity). The supply curve is the combination of the supply curves of a large number of producers, none of whom individually can change the supply curve.

Total Product:
the quantity of output

FIGURE 8.1

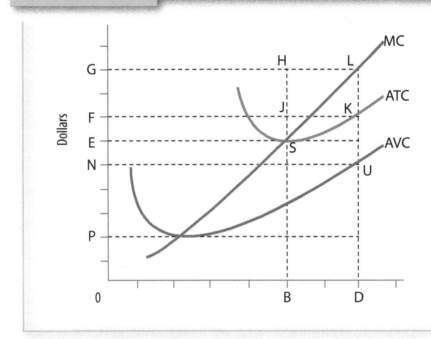

COMPETITIVE SUPPLY AND DEMAND RELATIONSHIPS,
INDUSTRY AND FIRM

Consider the following purely competitive supply and demand relationships in Figure 8.1 (above) representing an industry and a firm.

The combination of individual demand and supply relationships results in the industry demand and supply line. The industry equilibrium or market clearing price and quantity is where the total quantity demanded is equal to the total quantity supplied. The first graph in Figure 8.1 illustrates an industry equilibrium price of $3 and an industry equilibrium quantity of 300. This is typical of an increasing cost industry where costs increase as quantity supplied increases.

Notice that for the individual producer, price is perfectly elastic (horizontal demand) and is determined by the industry market. Any supplier pricing above the market price will have no sales and pricing below the market price is not logical.

THE INDIVIDUAL COST AND REVENUE RELATIONSHIPS

Price, marginal revenue, and average revenue are the same value.

$$P = MR = AR$$

Given the supply and demand Figure 8.1, an individual producer would have the following cost data:

Variable costs are costs that vary directly with the amount of output. When a manufacturer increases output, there will be increased costs with output for variables such as labor, materials, and shipping costs. As more units are produced, the total variable costs increase. Variable costs at a pepper food plant would include water, plants, fertilizer and labor.

Average costs: Economists also analyze the average costs (costs per unit of output). By finding the total cost and dividing by the number of units produced, average or per-unit costs are found.

TABLE 8.2

P	Q	Total Revenue	Average Revenue	Marginal Revenue
$3	0	$0	0	
				$3
$3	1	$3	$3	
				$3
$3	2	$6	3	
				$3
$3	3	$9	3	
				$3
$3	4	$12	3	
				$3
$3	5	$15	3	

Notice in Figure 8.2 that price always remains the same. Price and average revenue as well as marginal revenue remain equal. The addition of one more sale will increase average revenue and marginal revenue by the same amount as the price.

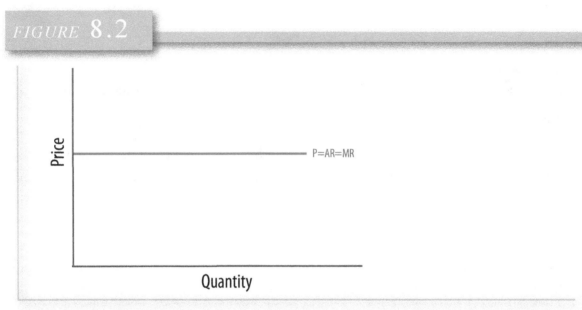

FIGURE **8.2**

RELATIONSHIPS OF PRICE, AVERAGE REVENUE, AND MARGINAL REVENUE

METHODS OF FINDING MAXIMUM PROFIT IN PURE COMPETITION

There are two methods of finding the maximum profit and related output for a firm:

- The total revenue approach
- The marginal approach

TOTAL REVENUE APPROACH

The **total revenue approach** simply finds total revenue (price times quantity) and subtracts total cost (ATC × quantity) resulting in profit or loss at each output level. The maximum profit output is where the difference between total revenue and total cost is the greatest. Recall that economic costs include a normal profit, and an economic profit is a profit greater than normal. A profit of $0 is a normal profit and a profit greater than $0 is an economic profit.

Economic Profit = Total Revenue (Price x Quantity)
minus Total Economic Costs

Consider the following pure competition application of a total revenue approach.

TABLE 8.3

P	Q	TR	ATC	TC	Profit
$80	1	$80	$150	$150	−$70
80	2	160	110	220	−60
80	3	240	90	270	−30
80	4	320	80	320	0
80	5	400	90	450	−50

The profit for each output level is the TR − TC. The maximum profit is found at a quantity of four units with a profit of $0 (meaning a normal profit since all costs including profit are compensated).

A check of the total revenue approach can be made by the average cost approach. In this method, average cost is compared to price. The firm should produce where the profit per unit multiplied by quantity is the highest. The point of maximum profit is where the price minus ATC multiplied by quantity is at a maximum value. In Table 8.3, subtracting the price of $80 from each ATC multiplied by quantity will result in a negative at each output point except at Q = 4 where there is a 0, meaning a normal profit. Thus, Q = 4 yields the maximum profit.

The Marginal Approach

In the **marginal approach** a firm will produce as long as a profit exists or losses are less than fixed costs. In order to maximize profit, the purely competitive firm will operate where the marginal revenue is equal to the marginal cost if, at this intercept, the price is greater than the average variable cost (AVC). In order to minimize losses, minimum average variable costs must be covered by price.

With MR of each additional unit greater than MC, firms will produce until MR = MC if this value is greater than the minimum AVC. If a competitive firm is producing where **MR is (greater than) > MC and MR is (greater than) > AVC**, the firm will increase profits or reduce losses by increasing production.

If MR is less than MC, less production is in the producer's best interest. If a firm is producing where **MR is < (less than) MC and MR is (greater than) > AVC**, the firm will increase profits or reduce losses by decreasing production.

When price is less than the minimum of the AVC, the supplier should produce zero units of output because the fixed cost loss is less than the operating loss. If a firm is producing where MR (P) (is less than) <AVC, output should be cut to zero. This is called the **shut down case**, where no production results in less loss than a producing loss.

TABLE 8.4

P	Q	TR	ATC	TC	MC	Profit
$80	1	$80	$150	$150		−$70
					$70	
80	2	160	110	220		−60
					$50	
80	3	240	90	270		−30
					$50	
80	4	320	80	320		0
					$130	
80	5	400	90	450		−50

The data from the previous problem can be reworked for the marginal approach. Since the MR is the price, MR = $80 and = MC at **4 units**. Notice that the MC data is between points and therefore the intercept with MR will be on a line with quantity. The quantity is 4 and the profit at 4 is TR − TC. TR = 4 × $80 = $320 and TC at 4 is $320 for a profit of $0. This is the same result as found using the total revenue approach.

FIGURE **8.3**

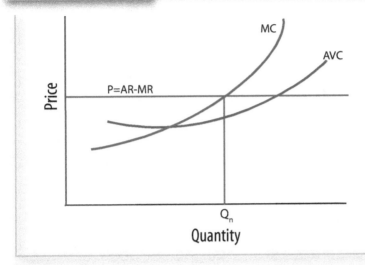

Graphic of Marginal Approach

In Figure 8.3, the firm will produce at Qn where MR (P) = MC because price is greater than the minimum of the AVC curve at the MR = MC intercept.

PURE COMPETITION, AN INDIVIDUAL IN THE SHORT RUN

FIGURE **8.4**

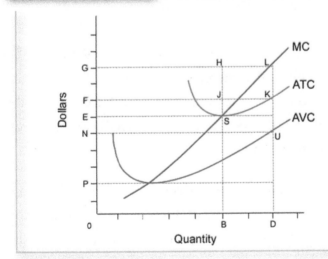

Graphic Approach to Finding Maximum Profit

These same principles can be applied by graphic rectangles to find maximum profit. The total revenue rectangle (P/Q where MR = MC) minus the total cost rectangle (ATC @ Q) = total profit rectangle (total revenue rectangle minus total cost rectangle).

GRAPHIC APPROACH TO FINDING MAXIMUM PROFIT

FIGURE 8.5

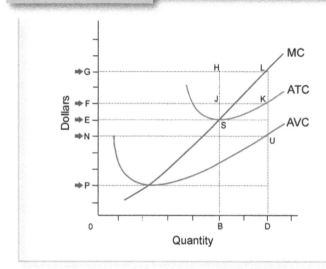

A Labeled Graphic Application

In the Figure 8.5 there are five prices: (➤) P, N, E, F, and G. The intercept of marginal revenue (price) with marginal cost determines a profit maximization point for price and quantity.

Using the letter labels on the graph, a firm with these costs and revenue at a price of G would produce at Quantity D because this is the intercept where MC = MR. The cost rectangle is determined by finding the quantity intercept with the ATC curve. At this price of G the total revenue box is GLOD, the total cost box is FKOD, and the profit rectangle is GLOD minus FKOD resulting in GLFK.

Using the same graph and a price of E the total revenue box is ESOB (the area that represents E multiplied by B or price times quantity), the total cost box is ESOB and the profit box is ESOB minus ESOB meaning there is no economic profit but only a normal profit.

FIGURE 8.6

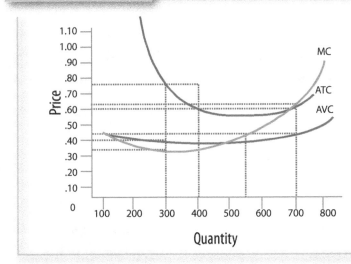

GRAPHIC APPROACH TO FINDING MAXIMUM PROFIT

A Quantitative Graphic Example

The marginal approach can be applied to a firm with costs as illustrated in Figure 8.6. MR = MC @ $.65 where the firm would choose quantity = 700 units to maximize profits. When the price is $.65, total revenue will be 700 times $.65 = $455 and total cost is 700 times $.60 = $420, leaving an economic profit of $35 ($455-$420).

BENEFITS OF PURE COMPETITION

There are benefits of pure competition for society and consumers. In the long run there can be no economic profit in pure competition and therefore, suppliers will produce at the lowest possible cost assuring consumers the lowest possible prices. Efficiency is assured to society because production must be at the lowest cost.

Within pure competition there is maximum societal and consumer benefit achieved as envisioned by Adam Smith in the invisible hand concept. Because of maximum competition, the lowest costs to consumers are realized with efficiency of resource use.

Disadvantages of Pure Competition

Within pure competition there is pressure to minimize costs and this may result in market failures such as spillover costs. A spillover cost is a cost that is incurred by those not a part of a market activity. Spillover costs may occur when a firm pollutes in order to reduce operating costs. For example, when farmers pollute the air or water, consumers of the product may have lower prices but society at large is forced to incur the spillover cost.

The final disadvantage of pure competition is that resources are allocated without consideration of social need. Each producer or buyer realizes benefit based upon their productive involvement. Individuals unable to contribute productive output will receive no market benefit.

Pure Competition Short Run to Long Run

In the long run, purely competitive firms can vary all of the factors of production: land, labor, capital, and entrepreneurship. Within the short run (with a fixed capacity) a firm may make a profit, loss, or a normal profit. However, profits or losses disappear in the long run because there are no barriers to entry or exit for firms. When a profit is realized other firms will come into the market and when there is a loss, firms will leave the market. Thus, in the long run, firms will operate where price = the minimum of the long run average total cost. Each firm must have sufficient economies of scale to reach the minimum cost in the long run but each firm must not encounter diseconomies of scale causing costs to rise above the minimum of the long-run average total cost curve.

Each competitive firm must operate in the long run at the optimum point quantity (Qn) to survive. Where P = ATC, there is no economic profit, only a normal profit, Figure 8.7.

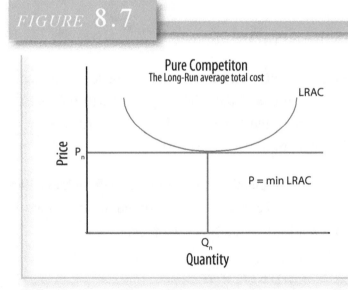

FIGURE 8.7

Pure Competiton
The Long-Run average total cost

LRAC

P_n

P = min LRAC

Q_n
Quantity

Price

THE LONG-RUN EQUILIBRIUM OF A PURELY COMPETITIVE FIRM

Conclusion

Pure competition represents the ultimate of competitive allocation and thereby the most efficient market model. Consumers receive the lowest costs in the long run because entry is open to other firms and short-term profits as well as losses will be driven away.

REAL WORLD ECONOMICS

HOW "PURELY COMPETITIVE" IS FARMING?

Although an individual farmer is often cited as operating in pure competition, in the real world of economics, the farm is often far from pure competition.

According to United States trade representatives at recent General Agreement on Tariffs and Trade (GATT) negotiations, current farm subsidies for both Europe and the United States are $200 billion each. These subsidies keep cheaper farm products from Europe and the United States. The Uruguay Round of GATT trade negotiations tried for many years to reduce these subsidies but because of politics and political lobbies, subsidies were not reduced.

The public interest group, Environmental Working Group (EWG), concluded:

> "The Top Ten Beneficiaries nationally include state governments, several universities, and individuals with interests in large farming operations, all of whom are projected to receive in excess of $600,000 in direct payment subsidies over the next five years if Congress maintains the status quo for this program.

Big Farm Businesses Will Reap Millions

Like other crop subsidies, direct payments are linked to production (acreage and per-acre yield). The larger the farming operation, the greater the direct payment subsidies it stands to receive.

If Congress extends the direct payment subsidies with no reforms, taxpayers will be sending millions of dollars to some of the largest, wealthiest farming operations in America, even if they are making record incomes as a result of high market prices."

Although most farmers do not receive direct payment subsidies, the government does directly intervene in the market for pricing, acreage set aside programs, and insurance coverage. These interventions clearly are contrary to a purely competitive market where diseconomies of scale would force inefficient producers out of business in the long run.

Pure Competition is a market model with the highest degree of competition and greatest resource efficiency.

Perfect Competition is a theoretical market model with perfect mobility of resources and perfect market information throughout the world.

Monopolistic Competition is a market model with strong emphasis on branding often associated with retail units.

Oligopolistic Competition is a market model with few competitors and much interdependency among units; often associated with the airline industry.

Monopoly is a market model with least competition where there is only one producer and no substitutes; often associated with a utility such as a municipal water unit.

Perfectly Elastic Demand Line is a horizontal demand line graphed parallel to the x-axis often associated with pure competition where marginal revenue is equal to price.

Total Revenue Approach is a method of finding maximum profit and output position by finding total revenue and subtracting cost at each output to locate the highest profit position.

Marginal Revenue Approach is a method of finding the maximum profit and output position by finding where marginal revenue (price) is equal to marginal cost above the average variable cost.

Supply Line of a Purely Competitive Firm is the line where marginal cost and marginal revenue intercept above the minimum of the average variable cost.

Spillover Costs are costs forced upon others outside the buyer and seller agreement.

Long Run Average Total Cost Curve of Pure Competition reaches a minimum where it is equal to price; therefore, there can be no economic profit in the long run within this model.

APPLIED EXERCISES

EXERCISE 1 :

Assume a Price = $10 and a min. A.V.C. of $5, what is the max. profit output and the amount of profit at that level?

QUANTITY	TOTAL COST
0	$25
1	35
2	41
3	45
4	47
5	49
6	52
7	57
8	65
9	79
10	120

APPLIED EXERCISES

EXERCISE 2 :

Mark each of the following statements True or False

_____ 1. In maximizing profit a firm will always produce that output where total revenues are at a maximum.

_____ 2. In the short run a competitive firm will always choose to shut down if product price is less than the lowest average total cost.

_____ 3. After all long-run adjustments have been completed, a firm in a competitive industry will produce that level of output where average total cost is at a minimum.

_____ 4. The long-run supply curve for a decreasing cost industry is downsloping.

_____ 5. A competitive firm will produce in the short run so long as its price exceeds its average fixed cost.

_____ 6. Marginal cost is a measure of the alternative goods which society foregoes in using resources to produce an additional unit of some specific product.

_____ 7. Price and marginal revenue are identical for an individual purely competitive seller.

_____ 8. Because the equilibrium position of a purely competitive seller entails an equality of price and marginal costs, competition produces an efficient allocation of economic resources.

_____ 9. The short run supply curve slopes upward because producers must be compensated for rising marginal costs.

_____ 10. The demand curve for a purely competitive industry is perfectly elastic, but the demand curves faced by individual firms in such an industry are down sloping.

_____ 11. Total revenue of a competitive seller graphs as a straight, up sloping line.

_____ 12. Marginal revenue is the addition to total revenue resulting from the sale of one more unit of output.

_____ 13. In a purely competitive industry, competition centers more on advertising and sales promotion than price.

_____ 14. Individual firms in purely competitive industries are price takers and not price makers.

_____ 15. If fixed cost loss from not operating is less than operating losses, the firm will not produce.

EXERCISE **1** :

Quantity	Total Cost	Total Revenue	Profit	Marginal Cost
0	$25	0		10
1	35	10	-25	6
2	41	20	-21	4
3	45	30	-15	2
4	47	40	-7	3
5	49	50	1	3
6	52	60	8	5
7	57	70	13	8
8	65	80	15	14
9	79	90	-11	41
10	120	100	-20	

A.   Working the problem as a total revenue approach, the maximum profit is $15 at 8 units of output.

B.   Working the problem as a marginal approach, the MR = P of $10 that is more than the minimum AVC of $5, therefore the firm should produce where MR = MC. This occurs at 8 units because the MR at 7.5 is 8 and 14 at 8.5 therefore the maximum profit is between at 8 units. Profit = Price × quantity – Total Cost or $10 × 8 = $80 minus Total Cost at 8 units = $65 therefore the profit is $15.

C.   Both approaches find the same output and profit position.

EXERCISE **2** :

The following numbers are False: 1, 2, 5, 10, 11, and 13

PURE MONOPOLY

INTRODUCTION

What is a monopoly? A pure monopoly is a firm producing a good/service with no substitutes. Since there is only one supplier, the firm is the industry and the firm is a price maker. Defined in this manner, there are few pure monopoly firms since most products/ services have substitutes. An example of a monopoly is a newly patented medication granted monopoly status by government.

LEARNING OBJECTIVES

Please note the listed objectives. As you will see, the course materials are all objective driven. This provides you with a constant way to direct and monitor your progress throughout the course.

1 OBJECTIVE ONE

Define "pure monopoly" and describe the economic characteristics of the monopoly model.

2 OBJECTIVE TWO

Given a TABLE of price and demand information, explain the effect of elasticity on a monopoly's decision to produce.

3 OBJECTIVE THREE

Use a graph of cost and revenue information to determine the optimum levels of output and pricing for a monopoly in a short-run model.

4 OBJECTIVE FOUR

Given a TABLE of demand information, explain the effect of profit on a monopoly's decision to produce.

5 OBJECTIVE FIVE

Describe the common misconceptions about monopolies and the actual inefficiencies that monopolies can represent.

I INTERACTIVE EXERCISE

Describe the types of regulation and long-run conditions that monopolies encounter.

CHARACTERISTICS OF THE MONOPOLY MODEL

Monopoly is made possible because of barriers that block competition from entering the market. Barriers that create monopoly include:

Economies of Scale

High costs of entry may effectively block competitors because average costs decrease with increasing volume. A natural monopoly exists where production has substantial economies of scale. Natural monopoly is sometimes present in public utilities allowed by government in order to have only one supplier with lower average total costs.

In the short-run average total cost (SRAC) curve in Figure 9.1, society could allow one producer at Q1 and ATC1 or two producers at Q2 at ATC2 or even 3 producers at Q3 at ATC3. As more producers are added, the efficiency is reduced because of lack of economies of scale. Under such conditions, a monopoly can lead to lower prices.

FIGURE 9.1

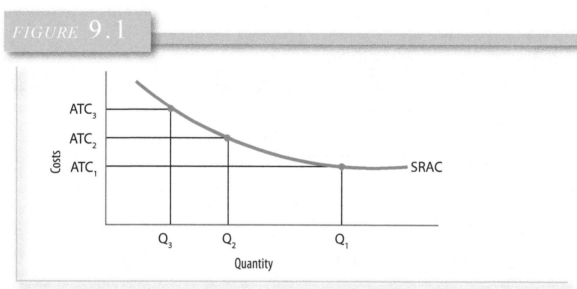

SHORT-RUN AVERAGE TOTAL COST OF THE NATURAL MONOPOLY CONDITION

Legal Barriers

Government grants monopoly status to firms through copyrights, patents, and licenses as a reward for an innovation or invention. This monopoly protection allows producers a set period of time with no competition.

Ownership of Essential Resources

Some firms have control of natural resources that are limited and necessary to make a product. Such a case creates monopoly power as was found in the aluminum industry.

Unfair Competition

Both dumping (selling below cost of production) or reciprocation arrangements (when firm A is forced to buy from firm B in order to sell to firm B) create monopoly conditions for a firm. These business arrangements are anti-competitive and are in violation of the Sherman Antitrust Act passed by Congress in 1890 and other more recent federal or state laws.

Economies of Being Established

Firms gain an economic benefit that may create monopoly power simply by being in business longer or being better known than competitors. Monopoly power is greater the more perceived uniqueness of the product.

Why Study Monopoly Model?

Although there are few pure monopoly firms, the analysis of pure monopoly is important to judge the behavior of firms having nearly monopoly status. Firms with more than 50% of the market can often be explained in part through the monopoly market model.

Cost Structures in Monopoly

The cost structures of a monopoly have the same relationship between fixed costs, variable costs, marginal costs, and average cost values as pure competition. A monopoly, like a purely competitive producer, has the same forces determining costs.

Time, Technology, and Monopoly

Barriers to competition are often challenged over time through technology. This was present with the breakup of monopoly power within the telephone communication industry (ATT), the computer manufacturing industry (IBM), the camera/film industry (Eastman Kodak), and the cable television firms with satellite television. Technological forces may move a monopoly firm into a more competitive model.

MONOPOLY DEMAND CURVE

The monopolist's demand curve is the same as the market demand for the product. A monopolist is a price setter but in order to sell a higher quantity, the monopolist must reduce price. The extent of the price reduction depends on cost relationships and price elasticity.

Maximum Profits in Monopoly

A monopoly will maximize profit by setting output at the point where MR = MC. There is a separation between the demand line (P/Q) and MR.

TABLE 9.1

Price	Quantity	Total Revenue	Marginal Revenue
$11	0	$0	$10
10	1	$10	8
9	2	18	6
8	3	24	4
7	4	28	2
6	5	30	0
5	6	30	-2
4	7	28	

Notice in the table above that in order to sell two units the producer had to reduce price from $10 to $9 for both purchasers. Therefore, the marginal revenue is less than the price (MR < P). The demand line (P/Q) is more than the MR curve because the marginal revenue reflects the fact that prices had to be reduced for all purchasers and not just the one who will only purchase at the reduced price. The firm would not logically produce in the inelastic segment of the demand line found at a price decrease from $5 to $4.

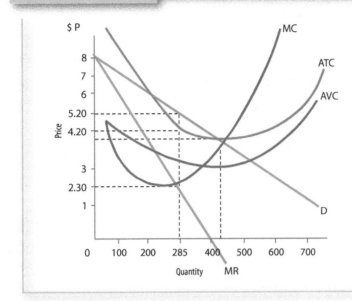

MONOPOLY

Monopoly Graph

A monopoly graph is displayed in **Figure 9.2**. Marginal revenue (MR) is less than price at every point except the initial point. Since the MR and P are different lines, the intercept of MR and marginal cost (MC) is below the demand line. To find the maximum profit output, locate where MR = MC and drop down to the quantity at that intercept on the x-axis. But to determine price at that quantity, a line must drawn from the maximum profit quantity to the demand line and then to the price on the y-axis. Remember the demand line is the price/quantity relationship. In the above, MR = MC at Q = 285 and the price from the demand line at 285 is $5.20.

To find the profit given a maximum profit output of 285 and price of $5.20, total revenue is found and total cost is subtracted. Total revenue is (285 multiplied times $5.20) = $1482 minus total cost (285 multiplied times $4.20) of $1197 resulting in a profit of $285.

Price Discrimination and Monopoly

Monopolists can increase their profits if they are able to discriminate on prices, in other words, charge different prices for the same item. Price discrimination is taping the demand line, meaning charging each customer the maximum they would be willing to pay without any consumer surplus.

In order for price discrimination to occur, the firm must have sufficient monopoly power to control both the price and output. In addition, the firm must be able to separate groups of buyers and keep them apart to prevent resale.

Price discrimination occurs in many firms such as with airline ticketing. Different prices are changed for the same seat according to when the ticket is purchased. Another example is when prices are discounted for students or seniors citizens.

Consider the following example of price discrimination:

TABLE 9.2

Price	Quantity Demanded
$100	0
80	1
60	2
40	3
20	4

With a non-price discriminating monopolist, at an output level quantity of three, the total revenue is $120 (Q multiplied by P) or 3 times $40 = $120. But if this firm is able to perfectly price discriminate, the total revenue when three units are sold is (1 @ 80 + 1 @ 60 + 1 @ 40) or $80 + 60 + 40 = $180. When markets are segmented, total revenue rises for the firm.

Societal Efficiency versus Monopoly Profit

Notice in Figure 9.2, the minimum of the ATC curve is where average revenue = marginal cost (AR = MC). However, the firm will operate for maximum profit at the quantity where MR = MC. The quantity supplied by monopolists is not the most efficient point or lowest cost point on the ATC. Society seeks for monopolists to operate at the point where AR = MC, with a lower price and lowest cost output than the MR = MC price/output level.

Monopolies generally are able to restrict output because of their market power position established through entry barriers. Monopolists are more likely to gain an economic profit than other market models.

FIGURE 9.3

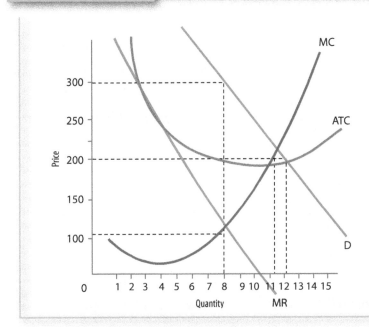

GRAPH OF MONOPOLY PRICE, COST RELATIONSHIP

Monopolies have the highest profit output where MR = MC and not where AR = MC.

Test Yourself with Data in Figure 9.3

Find the maximum profit and associated quantity for the firm in Figure 9.3. MR = MC at Q = 8. The maximum profit price is at $300 because at a quantity = 8, the price intercept is $300 bounced off the demand line. Since quantity = 8 and price equals $300, the total revenue is $2,400. The cost of producing quantity = 8 is found by locating the intercept of Q = 8 with the ATC line and this is at $200 per unit. Therefore the cost is $200 times 8 or $1,600. Total revenue is $2,400 less total cost of $1,600 leaving a profit of $800. Another approach is to find the price minus ATC = profit per unit times quantity. Price is $300; ATC is $200 with a profit of $100 per unit times a quantity of 8 or a profit of $800.

A MONOPOLY HAS NO SUPPLY CURVE

There is no supply curve possible when a downward sloping demand line separates price from marginal revenue. Therefore, there is no supply curve with any model other than pure competition that has a horizontal demand line.

Cost Inefficiencies in Monopoly

Cost inefficiencies may exist in monopoly because of:

Operating Inefficiency

Monopolies often incur higher costs because they are not competitive. For example, a monopoly firm may allow less efficient workers to be employed and pay workers more than the market rate. Monopolies tend to compensate workers at a higher rate than in purely competitive markets.

Risk Avoidance Behavior

Monopolies tend to avoid risk because they do not want to launch new products that might compete with their own market share.

Income Concentration

Monopoly power promotes inequality. Monopolies charge a higher price and this increases income for higher income individuals owning monopoly firms.

Rent Seeking Behavior

Rent seeking behavior exists when consumers are actually paying a periodic fee to a monopoly for use of a good or service. These market conditions may be allowed by government but add no value to the consumer. For example, some brand drugs charge a premium but are the same as generic drugs.

Costs of Government Regulation

Monopolies are often required to incur costs for public relations, lobbying, and legal fees to maintain their barriers. Most monopolies are monitored by government and may find it advantageous to maintain expensive political relationships. These costs are passed on to consumers.

Monopolies are visible to the public because of the lack of competition as well as the fact that they are more likely to have an economic profit. Therefore government is often encouraged by the public to regulate monopolies.

THE RESULTING DILEMMA OF REGULATION

Given the economic cost relationships of monopoly, government can mandate a price of the ATC to assure a fair-return price (price will cover per unit costs) or a price equal to the MC that is the minimum ATC. Each of these mandated prices involves an economic problem that is called the dilemma of regulation.

The socially optimal price (P = MC) achieves efficiency of allocation but may result in losses; the fair-return price (P = ATC) yields a normal profit but may fall short of allocation efficiency.

The amount of economic inefficiency with a monopoly may actually be less than the problems associated with government ownership of monopoly industries or even with a high degree of government regulation. Economists have long debated the inefficiency of monopolies but the actual loss of efficiency may sometimes be minor or even unavoidable. As more monopoly industries are deregulated, more competition has not generally decreased costs or prices. Because of the role of technology, there are more available substitutes for customers and some degree of competition exists in many partial monopolies.

Conclusion

In the long run, monopoly firms will often move toward normal profits because economic profits will attract resources trying to overcome monopoly barriers. While an economic profit is more likely in monopoly, technology and competitive factors may break down the barriers.

Also, mergers and consolidations may group competing resources and create a new power base to challenge monopoly. Horizontal mergers are direct competitors merging into one company. Vertical mergers are different production levels combining into one company (a peanut butter manufacturing firm buying a peanut farm). These forces bring a dynamic environment to challenge monopoly power.

DOES MONOPOLY REALLY EXIST IN AMERICAN MARKETS?

Monopoly became real world when a major firm was charged with illegal monopoly practices. In 1998 the United States Department of Justice (DOJ) along with 20 states filed a lawsuit against Microsoft Inc. (MS) for their operating systems and web browser business activities. Although Microsoft Inc. clearly was not the only producer of operating systems and web browsers, the court ruled that the market was effectively dominated and competition was blocked for other providers.

Microsoft Inc. argued that their products were clearly technologically more effective for consumers and this resulted in consumers choosing their products. MS further argued others were not barred from entry and in fact there was competition. The prosecutors, on the other hand, charged that the packaging of the Internet browser "Explorer" with the operating system blocked meaningful competition.

A number of well-known economists and legal experts testified for MS but an equal number argued for the DOJ. The element of competition versus technology and free markets became a centerpiece of the debate. The noted Nobel Prize winning economist Milton Friedman felt that any restriction by government in this case was setting a precedent for more unnecessary government regulation. (1)

In 2001, the DOJ reached an agreement with Microsoft Inc. The company agreed to limit its packaging of products and share "programming interfaces with third-parties." (2) The court tried to promote a balance between free markets and monopoly barriers.

This case is a classic example of the conflict between monopoly powers "destroying freedom of competition" compared to the barriers naturally present with technological success.

1   **Policy Forum:** The Business Community's Suicidal Impulse
2   **Microsoft Case**

Dilemma of Regulation is a condition within monopoly where price setting by government may result in greater efficiency but could result in monopoly losses.

Maximum Profit Output for a Monopoly is output where marginal revenue equals marginal cost.

Mergers are the combining of two or more firms into one company.

Natural Monopoly is a monopoly condition where economies of scale reduce costs so that only one producer is warranted.

Operating Inefficiency is a state where monopoly firms may not operate at lowest cost but accommodate higher costs due to market power such as paying higher salaries than competitive firms and passing on costs to consumers.

APPLIED EXERCISES

<u>EXERCISE</u> **1** :

Given the following data, find the maximum profit and maximum profit output using both the total revenue and marginal approaches.

QUANTITY	PRICE	TOTAL COST
0	16	$25
1	15	35
2	14	41
3	13	45
4	12	47
5	11	49
6	10	52
7	9	57
8	8	65
9	7	79
10	6	100

APPLIED EXERCISES

EXERCISE 2 :

Mark each of the following statements True or False

_____ 1. A monopolist is the sole producer of a commodity for which there is no close substitute.

_____ 2. Monopolies occur within the market because barriers keep competition away.

_____ 3. Monopolies are always less efficient than competitive firms.

_____ 4. Barriers to entry may allow a monopoly to maintain economic profits even in the long run.

_____ 5. Monopolists charge the highest price the market will bear.

_____ 6. High costs and a weak demand may prevent a monopoly from realizing a profit.

_____ 7. Monopolists avoid the inelastic segment of the demand line.

_____ 8. In general, a monopoly transfers income from consumers to owners of a monopoly because of rent seeking behavior of monopolies.

_____ 9. Economies of scale create a "natural monopoly."

_____ 10. Economies of scale may make lower unit costs available to monopolists but not to competitors.

_____ 11. Monopoly inefficiency is the failure to produce with the least costly combination of inputs.

_____ 12. Operating inefficiency is more common within a monopoly than in pure competition.

_____ 13. The barriers to entry present for a monopolist weakens the incentive to be technologically progressive.

_____ 14. Price discrimination is charging different prices by segmenting a market for the same item.

_____ 15. The perfectly discriminating monopolist will produce a larger output than the non-discriminating monopolist.

_____ 16. Price regulation can be used to force monopolists to produce more output.

_____ 17. The socially optimal price is determined where the demand and MC intersect.

_____ 18. The fair-return price is determined where demand and ATC intersect.

_____ 19. Monopolies always make a profit.

_____ 20. Monopolies are more likely to make a profit than are competitive producers

APPLIED EXERCISES: ANSWERS

EXERCISE 1 :

Price	Quantity	Total Revenue	Marginal Revenue	Total Cost	Marginal Cost	Profit
$16	0	0		$25		–$25
15	1	15	15	35	10	–20
14	2	28	13	41	6	–13
13	3	39	11	45	4	–6
12	4	48	9	47	2	1
11	5	55	7	49	2	6
10	6	60	5*	52	3*	8
9	7	63	3	57	5	6
8	8	64	1	65	8	–1
7	9	63	–1	79	14	-16
6	10	60	–3	100	21	-40

Maximum profit is shown at a price of $10 and 6 units

EXERCISE 2 :

True or False

False Statements: #3, 5, 15, 19

INTRODUCTION

The final two market models of microeconomics are monopolistic competition and oligopolistic competition. Along with monopoly, each of these models is considered as imperfect competition.

LEARNING OBJECTIVES

Please note the listed objectives. As you will see, the course materials are all objective driven. This provides you with a constant way to direct and monitor your progress throughout the course.

1 OBJECTIVE ONE

Identify the three models of imperfect competition and describe the general concept in terms of inefficiency, costs, and output.

2 OBJECTIVE TWO

Describe in detail the monopolistic competition model and provide "real world" examples of businesses in this imperfect competition.

3 OBJECTIVE THREE

Given a GRAPH of costs and revenue relationships, determine the optimum level of output and pricing for a monopolistically competitive firm.

4 OBJECTIVE FOUR

Discuss the inefficiencies of the monopolistically competitive firm from our society's point of view.

5 OBJECTIVE FIVE

Describe the oligopoly model using economic characteristics and provide "real world" examples of businesses in imperfect competition.

6 OBJECTIVE SIX

Discuss the advantages and disadvantages of oligopolies and the economic consequences of "Satisficing" (optimizing outcomes among all stakeholders such as owners, managers, and workers rather than maximizing profits).

Imperfect competition

Imperfect competition, as the name implies, is a model other than pure or perfect competition often having less efficiency, higher costs, and lower output than the maximum efficiency of pure competition.

Monopolistic Competition Is Not Monopoly

Monopoly and monopolistic competition must not be considered as the same. Each market model is unique and different. Monopolistic competition is competitive and is widely represented by retailing firms while monopoly has no competition and is comparable to some utility firms.

Characteristics of Monopolistic Competition

Monopolistic competition is described by a retail operation where there are many producers with similar products or services and many buyers. There is price competition as well as non-price competition. Non-price competition emphasizes the presentation of the good or service such as location. Within monopolistic competition, entry or exit is easy. Anyone may enter or leave the market freely. In addition, there is no likely collusion (agreements to set price and set market share among competitors).

Each of the features of monopolistic competition is readily identified by their uniqueness within an industry.

- Many firms are competing as in grocery stores.
- Product differentiation is present in fast food outlets.
- Non-price competition is typical of department stores.
- Easy entry and exit exists in the convenience stores industry.
- Similar products are present in bookstores.

Primary feature of monopolistic competition model: product differentiation

The most distinguishing feature of monopolistic competition is differentiation of the product or service. Product differentiation makes similar products different by meeting consumer needs in a customized manner. Product differentiation includes the presentation of products such as sales atmosphere, or location, service by employees, or some other features giving the goods and services a unique appeal. Retail stores make goods and services different by their marketing design. Expensive department stores market service and atmosphere. Inexpensive stores market location and expected lower prices or customer convenience such as check cashing services.

Applied Monopolistic Composition Models

Grocery stores are basically selling the same products, yet customers have a perceived reason why they shop at a given store. Location and ease of access is essential for grocery stores while department stores often have a loyal following because of their atmosphere. Convenience stores must have a readily accessible location but there is an open entry of competition.

A child with a lemonade stand is the ultimate example of ease of entry in monopolistic competition. Another child may enter as a competitor in the same area immediately. However, even with such simplification, the same economic mechanisms of economic allocation apply.

THE ECONOMIC RELATIONSHIPS OF MONOPOLISTIC COMPETITION

The monopolistic competition model of costs and revenue relationships are the same as monopoly as previously illustrated in Figure 9.2 and again here in Figure 10.1.

FIGURE 10.1

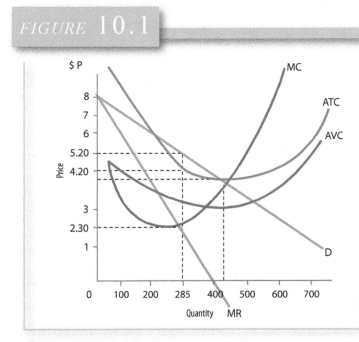

GRAPH OF MONOPOLY

The cost and revenue relationships in the monopolistically competitive model are the same as monopoly but for a different economic reason. Each model has the same graphic representation with the same basic price and quantity maximum profit outputs. Each model produces for maximum profits where MR = MC and each charges a higher price and produces less than the lowest cost output per unit (minimum of ATC).

Notice in the Figure 10.1 as with monopoly producers, the monopolistically competitive producers would produce where MR = MC. This same graph was presented in Figure 9.2. The maximum profit and related profit are the same as under monopoly with a quantity = 285, ATC = $4.20, price $5.20, and profit of $285. As with monopoly there is a higher price than desired by society and a lower quantity where AR = MC (quantity = 425).

THE INEFFICIENCY IN MONOPOLISTIC COMPETITION MODEL IS EXCESS CAPACITY

Monopolistically competitive producers will also operate at a higher point on the ATC curve than the minimum not because of barriers but because of excess capacity. Monopolistically competitive producers would be able to operate at lower costs if customers did not expect individualized, custom service, or an extensive array of products.

Monopolistic Competition Demand and Excess Capacity

Monopolistically competitive firms offer customers more services, a unique atmosphere and varied choices, resulting in higher costs. Higher costs can be seen in a retail outlet and this may cause us to wonder if we want lower costs with long lines, limited choices, and an austere atmosphere within stores. When rationing exists through lines or limited choices, customers will often be drawn to competing locations with greater customer service and better atmosphere, although higher prices. Retail outlets must adjust to customer expectations to add customer satisfaction.

The Role of Advertising in Monopolistic Competition

Advertising is an important feature of the monopolistically competitive market model. Since perceived or real product differences are important in monopolistically competitive markets, advertising is a means of relating advantages to customers.

Within the allocation of monopolistic competition, advertising:

- Stimulates product development (changes in the product to better meet consumer needs).

- Promotes competition.

- Provides information to consumers. National media is strongly supported by this model for most television, radio, and magazine advertising.

Many advertisers defend advertising expenditures as being economically viable to the market because these expenditures increase sales resulting in economies of scale and thus reduce consumer prices. This is not often correct as advertising generally increases prices and results in payments to individuals with higher incomes. Advertising is further challenged as promoting inefficient allocation of resources and monopoly power. However, consumers make choices on products and the value of advertising is decided through customer purchases.

Demand Elasticity of Monopolistic Competition Model

The demand elasticity of monopolistically competitive producers is determined by:

- The number of competing firms/outlets with similar products (the more outlets, the more elastic the price). For example, bottled water tends to be readily available at many locations and tends to be elastic to price.

- The customer perception of the similarity or uniqueness for the product/service. When consumers consider monopolistically competitive products as different, the good or service is less elastic; however, when goods are considered the same, the goods are more elastic to price. Brand name products tend to be more unique and thereby less price elastic.

Equilibrium in Monopolistic Competition

In the short run, all market models can operate at a profit, loss, or just a normal profit (no economic profit). When the ATC is above the price at the maximum profit quantity, the firm is incurring a short-term loss. In the longer term, this loss will be driven out by firms dropping out of the market and prices rising to meet total costs.

However, a firm will incur a profit in the short run if the price at the maximum profit quantity is above the ATC. Other firms recognize the profit in this model and, with easy entry, competitors will begin producing, driving down prices and driving out profits. In the long run, there will be an adjustment to a new equilibrium where TR = TC and only a normal profit will exist.

THE OLIGOPOLY MODEL

The final market model discussion is oligopoly; the term is derived from the Greek word *few*. Oligopoly is a market with few competing firms.

The oligopoly model is more difficult to analyze than other models because products may be identical (homogenous) or different (heterogeneous). Within a homogenous market there is more conformity to the economic theory of pure oligopoly. Homogeneity of products/services (standardized products) exists in steel or concrete production where the products are identical. Heterogeneity exists in other oligopoly markets such as automobiles, breakfast cereal, and tobacco.

The Concentration Ratio

Oligopoly is often a market with a few sellers supplying all or most of the total output in the industry. The degree of fewness is measured by the concentration ratio. The concentration ratio is the percentage of the market held by the top four producers. If a market has eight suppliers but the top four hold 70% of the total market, the industry is considered to be 70% concentrated. There is high market concentration in breweries, automobiles, and beer production, where the top four firms hold over 50% of the market.

The following concentration ratios were determined by the US Department of Commerce in 2002.

Manufacturing Group	Concentration Ratio
Tobacco	99.3
Breweries	90.8
Breakfast Cereal	92.1
Military Armored Vehicles	99.3
Motor Vehicles	91.2
Household Vacuum Cleaners	77.9
Pesticide and Agriculture Chemicals	64.5

Concentration Ratios: 2002 Economic Census Manufacturing Subject Series Issued May 2006 kEc02-32Sr-1—US Census Bureau— US Dept of Commerce, Economics and Statistics Adm.

The Characteristics of Oligopoly

Economies of Scale Restrict the Number of Producers.

The existence of economies of scale often requires large output to allow for lower costs. Firms may have economies of scale because of high startup costs such as in automobile manufacturing.

Ownership of Raw Materials May Be Held by Few Firms.

In some oligopolistic markets a few firms control the resources to produce the products as was the case with the wholesale diamond market.

Advertising May Be Too Costly for Many Producers.

Extensive advertising expenditures may restrict the market to those able to afford such high costs. This is present with some consumer products such as soap products where brand identification is important.

Government Restrictions May Exist on the Number of Producers.

Government may grant firms the right to license their patented product to produce through other firms. This allows only those licensed by the inventor access to the market.

Price Stability

Because there are few firms in an oligopoly industry, each firm is interdependent upon the other for price. In a standardized oligopoly, a change in price by one will significantly impact the others. Given the economic nature of this relationship, suppliers are more likely to avoid price wars (intense price cutting) and follow a price leader.

Oligopoly Strategy

The economic and logical position of a firm in an oligopoly market can be analyzed through game theory. Game theory is a model for valuing expected results from different business strategies. This system suggests that firms in oligopoly are more profitable with cooperation among their rivals. By having a low price, others would match the price and the advantage would no longer exist. By having a high price, few buyers would purchase from this firm. Therefore, the firm is well advised not to follow a high price or low price strategy but rather to cooperate with other producers in maintaining the price within a moderate zone.

Price Leadership in Oligopoly

Oligopoly firms will infrequently change prices, but with an increase in costs, a price leader may increase prices and others will follow. In the airline industry Southwest Airlines Inc. tends to have their prices watched and often followed by competitors. Overall price changes are infrequent in the airline industry but often occur following changes in fuel cost.

The Collusive Nature of Oligopoly

Internationally, the oligopoly model exists in many nations that allow firms to set market price and set market share. Such an arrangement is called collusion and if in writing, called a cartel. Collusion is illegal in the United States. However, consumers in the United States can be impacted by operations of cartels outside the United States as in the oil cartel. Since American laws do not apply in other nations, global cartels may influence American prices.

Price arrangements between oligopoly firms do exist in the United States, but are of a subtle nature through observation or informal contracts between suppliers.

FIGURE 10.2

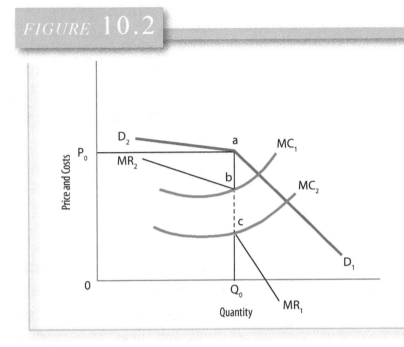

NON-COLLUSIVE OLIGOPOLY KINKED DEMAND

Within a non-collusive oligopoly, firms will tend to have cost and revenue relationships similar to the kinked demand model of oligopoly. The demand line actually consists of two lines; one is elastic above the prevailing price and the other is inelastic below the prevailing price. The intersection of the two lines forms an apex defining the price as in Figure 10.2.

Oligopoly Pricing Dilemma

Figure 10.2 illustrates that the demand line segment (D2 to a) is elastic above the existing price (Po) and inelastic below the existing price (a to D1). If a firm raises its price above the existing price, the demand line is elastic and therefore with an increase in price in the elastic area, total revenue goes down. The demand line is elastic above the existing price because other firms do not follow the price increase and buyers will purchase from the other suppliers with lower prices. The firm increasing price will be left alone with a higher price.

The demand line (a to D1) below the existing price (P0) is inelastic for all price decreases. With an inelastic demand and a price decrease, total revenue will decline. The demand line is inelastic below the industry price because firms will be forced to follow a price decrease and therefore, no single firm will benefit from lower prices.

Multiple Marginal Cost and Marginal Revenue Curves

Each oligopolistic firm will have a different marginal cost relationship represented between zones MC1 and MC2 in Figure 10.2. Because of the necessity of price agreement, the price/output is largely determined through market forces rather than intercepts with marginal cost and marginal revenue. Marginal revenue will break into two segments because of kinked demand with both D1 and D2 segments.

ADVANTAGES OF OLIGOPOLY

Oligopoly does offer advantages for firms requiring large capital investments. Firms must be assured of infrequent price changes and limited competition in order to make an expected return. Technology related manufacturing requires a large investment and much research and development to maintain a competitive operation. The oligopoly model does allow for more accommodation for these firms.

Disadvantages of Oligopoly

Critics of oligopoly argue that there is neither government control nor efficiency in this model. Firms in this industry according to critics can be inefficient and have fewer government restrictions than monopoly but maintain market power because of fewness.

With globalization, oligopoly industries such as steel, automobiles, and consumer products, are actually facing more competition with fewer informal pricing agreements. Firms have to make do.

Conclusions of Market Model Theories

Each of the four market models is a unique economic structure relative to the allocation of resources. Microeconomics provides an explanation for each firm's behavior. The advantages and disadvantages to buyers, sellers, and society can be better understood through microeconomic analysis.

Each firm however, operates within a complex set of demands and expectations by each of its constituents: consumers, employees, stockholders, bondholders, government, management, and board of directors. Business management must optimize the allocation of resources to satisfy all organizational components. Dr. Herb Simon won the Nobel Prize in Economics for his varied contributions to economic theory including the term "satisficing" that means pleasing all parties involved rather than just maximizing profit. A firm must optimize among it's choices.

Each economic model results in a degree of efficiency often thought by economists to be more efficient than a government operated monopoly. Although opinions vary on the degree of efficiency of each market, the existing systems do evolve. Monopoly power is challenged anew by both international and technological forces. The ability to be informed of market conditions and to move goods and services creates new opportunities for open markets, improved products, and lower prices.

REAL WORLD ECONOMICS

HOW ARE MARKETS AND ADVERTISING REGULATED?

In monopolistically competitive and oligopolistic environments, advertising is important in establishing and maintaining market share. Television viewers have all watched "questionable advertising" and wondered how such statements could be allowed. The question is, "who regulates?"

The Federal Trade Commission (FTC) is charged with regulating national markets for advertising. According to the FTC commissioner, advertising must be monitored by firms themselves, the media accepting advertising, and finally by the FTC. The commissioner quotes another commissioner as saying "we need to clean up the diet ad mess." There is an admission of regulation problems even among commissioners.

Advertising Guidance is provided by the FTC on their Website in selective areas including:

- Bait Advertising - advertising to get you "in the door"
- Deceptive Pricing
- Dietary Supplements
- Use of the Word "Free"
- Vocational and Distance Education Schools
- Weight Loss Products

The field of advertising must be filtered by everyone involved in the process. The consumer must be vigilant in screening what is realistic and buy accordingly, while firms must act responsibly.

Concentration Ratio is a penetration or percentage of the total market held by the largest four firms.

Game Theory is an evaluation of business strategy projecting profit outcomes.

Imperfect Competition is a competitive market situation that does not operate under the rules of pure competition including monopoly, monopolistically competitive, and oligopolistic models.

Kinked Demand Model has a line of a non-collusive oligopoly with elastic demand above existing price and inelastic below.

Monopolistic Competition is exemplified by retail stores where products are made appealing through product differentiation.

Non-price Competition is a means of competing on a basis other than price such as product differentiation.

Oligopoly is a model characterized by only a few producers with concentration such as automobile, steel, and oil industries.

Product Differentiation is the process of distinguishing similar products or services through customization such as store atmosphere, service, display, or access.

EXERCISE 1 :

Mark each of the following as True of False

_____ 1. A purely competitive seller's demand curve is elastic while the purely competitive industry is perfectly elastic.

_____ 2. In a purely competitive model an individual producer has marginal revenue = marginal cost = price = average revenue.

_____ 3. The elasticity of demand for an individual in purely competitive demand is perfectly elastic.

_____ 4. In the short run a purely competitive producer will produce if the price is greater than the minimum of the average variable cost.

_____ 5. In the short run a purely competitive producer may make a profit or a loss.

_____ 6. Monopolists make profits unlike a purely competitive producers.

_____ 7. A purely competitive producer will try to produce where total revenue is more than total cost by the largest amount.

_____ 8. In most models suppliers will seek to produce where MR = MC.

_____ 9. If a competitive firm has MC = AVC at $10, MC = ATC at $12, and MC = MR at $12; then the firm should not produce.

_____ 10. The kinked demand curve of an oligopoly is elastic above the market price.

_____ 11. In the long run, purely competitive producers tend to make a normal profit by operating where price = average total cost.

_____ 12. Monopolistically competitive producers maximize profits by producing where Average Revenue = Marginal Cost.

_____ 13. The demand curve of a purely competitive producer is less elastic than an imperfectly competitive producer.

_____ 14. The economic profits earned by monopolistically competitive producers tend to be positive in the long run.

_____ 15. Most firms in America tend to be purely competitive.

APPLIED EXERCISES

EXERCISE 2 :

Consider each market characteristic below and list at least one of the four market models: Pure Competition (PC), Monopolistic Competition (MC), Oligopoly (O), or Monopoly (M) for each of the following

1. The firm is the industry.

2. A profit in the long run is not possible.

3. Produces a differentiated product.

4. An interdependent market.

5. May have a "kinked demand."

6. A perfectly elastic demand line.

7. Has a supply line @ MC above the minimum AVC.

8. Is typical of the retail trade.

9. Has a separation of MR and P.

10. A profit in the long run is more possible than other models.

11. Is the most efficient of the models.

12. May have differentiated or standardized products.

13. Makes the most use of advertising.

14. Typical of oil, steel, and automobile manufacturers.

15. P = MR.

16. P = minimum of the LRATC.

17. MR = MC @ the decreasing ATC (not lowest).

18. Typical of the airline industry.

19. Products/services may be either homogenous or heterogeneous.

20. This model is often characterized by excess capacity.

EXERCISE 1 :

Answer: False statements: 1, 6, 9, 12, 13, 14, 15

EXERCISE 2 :

NUMBER	TYPE	DESCRIPTION
1	Monopoly (M)	The firm is the industry
2	Pure Competition (PC)	A profit in the long run is not possible
3	Monopolistic and Oligopoly (M,O)	A differentiated market
4	Oligopoly (O)	An interdependent market
5	Oligopoly (O)	May have a "kinked demand"
6	Pure Competition (PC)	A perfectly elastic demand line
7	Pure Competition (PC)	Has a supply line @ MC above the minimum AVC
8	Monopolistic Competition (MC)	Is typical of the retail trade
9	Monopoly, Monopolistic Competition, Oligopoly(M, MC, O)	Has a separation of MR and P
10	Monopoly (M)	A profit in the long run is more possible than other models
11	Pure Competition (PC)	Is the most efficient of the models
12	Oligopoly (O)	May have differentiated or standardized products
13	Monopolistic Competition (MC)	Makes the most use of advertising

14	Oligopoly (O)	Typical of oil, steel, and automobile manufacturers
15	Pure Competition (PC)	$P = MR$
16	Pure Competition (PC)	P = minimum of the LRATC
17	Monopoly, Monopolistic Competition, Oligopoly (M, MC,O)	$MR = MC$ @ the decreasing ATC (not lowest)
18	Oligopoly (O)	Typical of the airline industry
19	Oligopoly (O)	Products/services may be either homogenous or heterogeneous
20	Monopolistic Competition (MC)	This model is often characterized by excess capacity

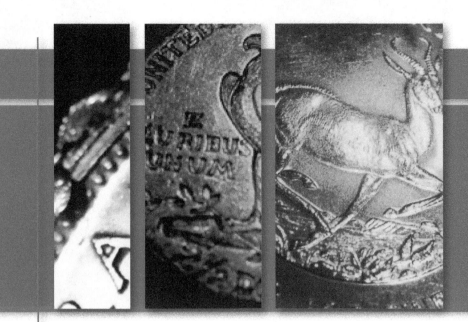
INTRODUCTION

The principles of resource allocation are discussed throughout the text but the most basic principle is the concept of cost/benefit analysis. This principle is applied in a modified form with marginal revenue to marginal cost, supply to demand, and marginal utility to price. Cost/benefit analysis is now applied to factor markets.

LEARNING OBJECTIVES

Please note the listed objectives. As you will see, the course materials are all objective driven. This provides you with a constant way to direct and monitor your progress throughout the course.

1 OBJECTIVE ONE

Identify the three models of imperfect competition and describe the general concept in terms of inefficiency, costs, and output.

2 OBJECTIVE TWO

Describe the theory of marginal productivity and the significance of the relationship between MFC and MRP.

3 OBJECTIVE THREE

Determine the optimum level of employment in an environment of pure competition by using a TABLE or GRAPH of cost and revenue information.

4 OBJECTIVE FOUR

Determine the optimum level of employment in an environment of imperfect competition by using a TABLE or GRAPH of cost and revenue.

5 OBJECTIVE FIVE

Describe the demand, substitution and complementary relationships that exist in the allocation of time by the individual worker.

6 OBJECTIVE SIX

Discuss the criticisms of the marginal productivity theory and the recent trends in US productivity.

Circular Flow Factor Model

The circular flow model, Figure 11.1 previously described in Lesson 1, illustrates the flow of resources from households to businesses for both the products market (at the top) and factor markets (at the bottom). Product markets exchange business production for sales receipts and factor markets exchange land, labor, capital, and entrepreneurship for rent, wages, interest, and profit respectively. This lesson analyzes factor market resource allocation.

FIGURE **11.1**

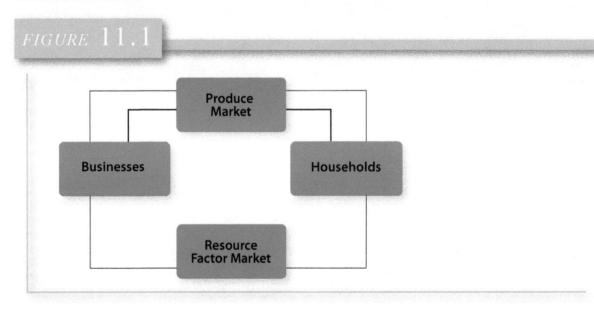

Factor market allocation for labor as well as land, capital, and entrepreneurship, is based upon the cost of the input relative to the contribution to output. The allocation process establishes what resources are used and this interplay among resources determines costs and income of factors.

Marginal Productivity Theory

The cost/benefit principle applied to factor markets concludes that a resource factor should be employed only if the marginal benefit is greater than the marginal cost, up to the point where the two are equal. The allocation of resources is determined by the owner of the resource input such as labor providing the supply, and firms providing the demand for factors.

When the allocation among the factors of production is combined in the most efficient manner, the highest value of input and output use is achieved. Each element receives an income according to their **contribution margin** or amount of revenue generated by its use. The system is best served when each input resource is used at its "highest and best use" occurring with the most output per input of resource cost.

Marginal productivity theory assumes income is a function of the contribution to output value (value added). If one resource input such as labor increases value output more than an equal amount of input cost from capital then more labor should be used. The adjustment among resource inputs results in the highest factor pay and lowest costs.

Derived Demand

The demand for most input resources is derived from the demand for the good it produces. The demand for the input resource is called a **derived demand.** For example, the demand for labor on a corn farm is derived from the demand for corn. The number of workers producing corn is directly related to productivity of all corn factor inputs (not just labor) and the demand for corn by consumers for food and even for energy. The demand for corn is the relationship between the prices of farm input factors (labor, interest cost, rent for land, profit of operation) and the quantity of corn demanded at various prices.

Derived demand is determined by the productivity (output/cost per input resource) and the market value of the good or services produced. Consider the simple firm output below with only one input (number of workers) in a competitive model. The competitive model assumes additional workers can be hired at the same additional cost and goods sold at the same price at all levels of output.

The competitive model illustrated in Table 11.1 is consistent with a short-run plant employing up to five workers. The number of workers employed is determined by the value added by each additional worker relative to cost. Since this is a competitive model, each additional worker costs the same and each additional product is sold for the same price of $3. The output is the number of goods produced; marginal product is the amount of additional goods produced by adding each additional worker and is represented at midpoint values. The addition of the first worker adds 10 units of output and is represented at .5 as the rate of additional output increasing from zero workers to one.

As more workers are hired past some point of input, additional output is subject to the law of diminishing returns with decreasing amounts of marginal product per additional worker. The total revenue is the output produced multiplied by the constant price of $3. The final column, marginal revenue product (MRP) is the change in the total revenue from each additional worker added.

TABLE 11.1

		PURELY COMPETITION FACTOR MODEL			
Worker	Output	Marginal Product	Produce Price	Total Revenue	Marginal Revenue Product
0	0		$3	$0	
1	10	10	3	30	$30
2	19	9	3	57	27
3	27	8	3	81	24
4	34	7	3	102	21
5	40	6	3	120	18

PURE COMPETITION, AN INDIVIDUAL IN THE SHORT RUN

$$\text{Marginal Revenue Product} = \frac{\text{Change in Total Revenue}}{\text{Change in input (number of workers)}}$$

Marginal Productivity Theory

Marginal productivity theory is the basis for efficient factor allocation. Each additional input resource should be added as long as it contributes a greater value (MRP) than the cost of adding the resource, the marginal factor cost (MFC), to the point where the two are equal. In order to maximize profits a firm would add additional workers when the MRP is greater than the MFC to the point where MFC = MRP.

$$\text{Marginal Factor Cost} = \frac{\text{Change in input Cost}}{\text{Change in input Quantity}}$$

The MRP forms the demand for the labor resource as shown in Table 11.1 and graphed in Figure 11.2. The demand for workers is determined by the value each worker adds to the marginal revenue product (MRP). Assuming that output is each priced at $3 and given the resulting marginal revenue product (MRP), the number of workers will be determined by the marginal factor cost (MFC). If the wage for each worker is $23, how many workers will be utilized? Given $23 as the MFC, the first, second, and third workers would be hired since they bring MRP values of $30, 27 and 24 respectively that are greater than $23. However, the fourth worker would not be hired since this worker would cost $23 but produce a value of only $21.

Demand is determined by the sovereign (independent) consumer. When a consumer purchases a product, a demand is created for this item to be re-stocked by the merchant. This idea is the origin of the saying, "the dollar votes when an item is bought." Consumer sovereignty determines what is produced in a capitalist economy.

FIGURE 11.2

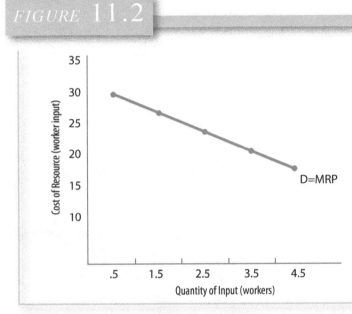

GRAPHIC APPROACH TO FINDING MAXIMUM PROFIT

Imperfect Competition

Marginal productivity theory is applied to imperfect markets (market models other than competitive) with similar inputs but varied output results. In an imperfectly competitive market, the cost of labor inputs and the price of the products will vary with market forces. Within a competitive market the MFC and the price of the product will remain constant. However, in an

> Demand is determined by the sovereign (independent) consumer

imperfectly competitive market, prices decrease to increase quantity demanded. With a decrease in price, the MRP drops more quickly from a higher level of output and results in fewer workers being hired. Consider the following imperfectly competitive model.

TABLE 11.2

IMPERFECTLY COMPETITIVE FACTOR MODEL

Worker	Output	Marginal Product	Produce Price	Total Revenue	Marginal Revenue Product
0	0		$4		
1	10	10	3.5	$35	$35
2	19	9	3.2	60.8	25.8
3	27	8	2.9	78.3	17.5
4	34	7	2.6	88.4	10.1
5	40	6	2.3	92	3.6

IMPERFECTLY COMPETITIVE FACTOR MODEL

FIGURE 11.3

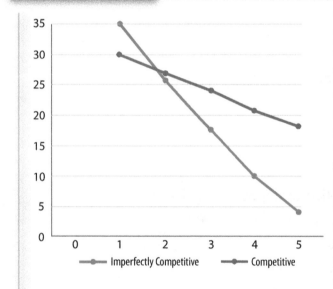

Imperfectly Competitive   Competitive

Table 11.2 and Figure 11.3 represent the MRP applied to an imperfect factor market. The price decreases as quantity increases. The marginal revenue product (MRP) is the change in the total revenue with the addition of one more worker. Again, the maximum profit occurs where MFC = MRP and will determine the number of workers hired. Given a MFC of $23, two workers would be hired because the MFC of $23 is less than $35 at one worker and also less than $25.80 at two workers, but $23 is more than $17.50 at three workers. Therefore at MFC = $23, two workers would be hired. However, at $23 in pure competition (previously calculated) three workers would be hired.

IMPERFECT DEMAND FOR LABOR

A Comparison of Competitive with Imperfectly Competitive Resource Demand

The demand for labor within a competitive firm is more responsive to decreases in the price of labor (MFC) than an imperfectly competitive firm. As prices drop for labor in a competitive firm, more labor resources are added than in imperfect competition. The imperfectly competitive producer is less likely to hire more labor because the price of the product drops with increases in output.

The demand curve of a competitive producer falls because of decreases in MP with increases in the number of workers. In an imperfectly competitive firm however, the demand falls because of decreases in product prices with increases in quantity as well as decreases in the MP with additional labor inputs.

FIGURE 11.4

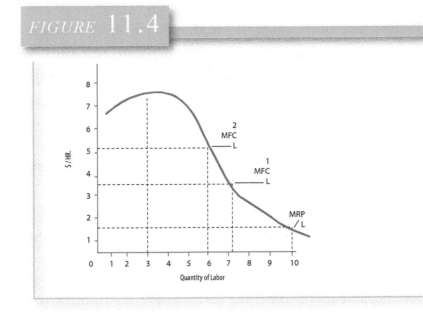

Labor Equilibrium Market Graphic Illustration

Given the above relationship of labor demand inputs (MRPL) and labor costs (MFCL), the firm would operate for maximum profit where the MFC = MRP (shown as MRPL = MFCL). Assuming MFCL1 is $3.50 per hour, the firm would hire seven workers but when MFCL2 is $5.00 per hour, only six workers would be hired.

The Shifting Demand for Factor Resources

The demand for resource factors of labor, land, entrepreneurship and capital depend upon the demand for the product, the productivity of each factor input (resulting in additional output), and the change in the price of the factor. The demand for wheat farmers depends upon the consumer demand for wheat as well as the productivity of each farmer compared to the productivity of capital equipment and fertility of land; each considered individually relative to output.

If the price of the labor, land, or equipment changes, then each element is subject to a shift in the demand for that factor of production. The factor allocation increases if the productivity of a factor increases and the value of that input increases MRP. If better trained farm labor results in higher output, labor services are of greater value or if new capital equipment is more efficient at less cost, the value of capital input increases. When input prices change, a firm may change the mix of input to reduce cost, even with the same output.

Changes in Resource Input Prices

Capital and labor are often **substitutable** for one another. If the price of labor increases, but all other factors remain the same, more capital will tend to be utilized to increase productivity of each worker. On the other hand, all other things remaining the same, if the price of capital decreases (the cost of equipment or even the interest rate for purchasing equipment), more capital will be used and **less labor**. Thus, capital and labor are substitutable resources and this process is called the **substitution effect.**

When a decrease in costs results in an increase in quantity demanded due to price sensitivity, the **output effect occurs.** For example, as the price of capital equipment decreases, costs and prices of the product decrease so more output units will be purchased. With decreases in costs and therefore prices, more workers will be employed to produce the larger quantity demanded of goods.

The difference between the substitution effect and the output effect is called the **net effect.** Since the substitution and output effect are opposites, the one with the greater value will determine the change. This value may have a positive impact (with more of the output effect) or negative impact (with more of the substitution effect) for labor demand.

The Demand for Labor

The total demand for labor depends upon the demand for the good/service (output effect), the productivity of labor compared to the productivity of capital (substitution effect), and the price of labor compared to the price of capital.

The demand for labor will increase if:

- there is an increase in the demand for the product using the labor.
- there is an increase in the productivity of labor (output to input or additional output per worker).
- there is a decrease in the price (cost) of labor.
- there is an increase in the price (cost) of capital.

A decrease in labor will occur if each of the above is reversed.

FIGURE 11.5

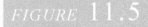

Graph of Demand for Labor

In initial equilibrium the demand for labor is shown in Figure 11.5.

FIGURE 11.6

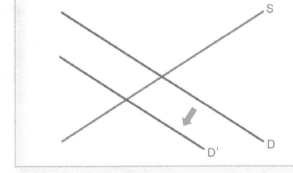

Decrease in Labor Demand

A decrease in demand for labor and constant supply shown in Figure 11.6 reduces both price and quantity demanded for labor. Such a left shift in demand might be caused by a decrease in the demand for the product, increase in the cost of labor, or a decrease in the cost of capital.

FIGURE 11.7

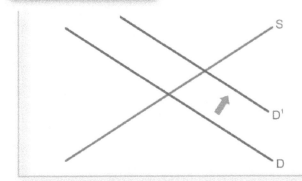

Increase in Labor Demand

With an increase in the demand for labor and constant supply the demand is shown in Figure 11.7. This movement might be caused by any of the changes described in insert A through D above. Such an increase in demand would increase both price and quantity demanded for labor.

The effect on demand for labor if workers increase their skills would be an increase in demand for labor. An opposite force could be illustrated by the effect on demand for labor if a decrease in the price of cars decreases the marginal revenue product of automobile workers resulting in a decrease in the demand for labor. A similar decrease in demand would occur if part of an automobile assembly line is automated.

Supply of Labor or Leisure

Individual workers will choose how they allocate their time when an increase in the demand for labor increases wages. The substitute effect for individual workers occurs when individuals decide to work more and consume less leisure thus increasing labor supply.

The income effect has the opposite impact on an individual worker. The income effect applies when individuals choose more leisure and work less (supply less labor) because leisure is a normal good made more affordable with a higher income.

When the substitution effect is greater than the income effect, wages increase the supply of labor. However, if the income effect is greater than the substitution effect the supply of labor decreases.

The Best Allocation of Capital and Labor

The most efficient combination of capital and labor together will determine the quantity of each used. The basic economic principle of cost/benefit analysis is applied to each factor of production. If the MP of labor divided by the cost of labor is greater than the MP of capital divided by the cost of capital, more labor should be employed as it increases output/cost more than capital/cost.

> Income effect applies when individuals choose more leisure and work less

$$\frac{\text{Marginal Product of Labor (MPL)}}{\text{Cost of Labor (Price)}}$$

$$\text{Equals}$$

$$\frac{\text{Marginal Product of Capital (MPC)}}{\text{Cost of Capital (Price)}}$$

Criticism of Marginal Productivity Theory

Although marginal productivity theory is a generally accepted principle of microeconomics, critics argue that the theory is not universally applied because of market failures. Within the real world, individuals are not always paid according to their marginal contribution because of the inability of an economy to fully utilize all workers at their highest and best use.

The marginal revenue product or contribution margin of each factor input is often difficult or impossible to compute within a dynamic system of many resource inputs.

For example, one might consider the value of labor compared to management or owners. Each entity is a necessity but difficult to value one compared to another. Many studies provide a historical comparison of the relationships, but the value of each specific unit at a point in time is controversial to say the least.

> Supply is the relationship between price and quantity supplied

FIGURE 11.8

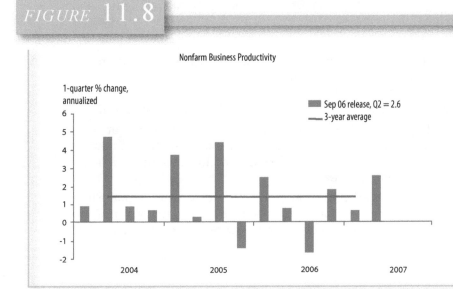

Source: bureau of labor statistics

Recent Productivity and the New Economy

In the last three years the non-farm business productivity has been at less than 2% on a three moving-year average. This is significantly less than the productivity average of the previous 10 years. The US economic growth in the late 1990s was more than half again as much as today. Many economists consider that in the late 1990s productivity gain was a result of increases in the effective use of technology. The aggregate supply and aggregate demand did increase in this period with decreases in unemployment and low inflation.

Although marginal productivity theory is difficult to apply, microeconomic principles identify the role of each production factor and its relationship with efficient use.

REAL WORLD ECONOMICS

HIGH EXECUTIVE COMPENSATION: MARKET OR MONOPOLY?

According to marginal productivity theory, each worker should be compensated according to his or her contribution to marginal revenue product. How does this apply to a chief executive officer (CEO) of a firm and how does American CEO compensation compare to global CEO compensation?

According to the Institute for Policy Studies, the average American worker pay adjusted for inflation remained the same from 1990 to 2004 while average executive pay rose from $2.82 million to $11.8 million.

Certainly the role of a CEO is important and this is true of firms throughout the world. According to *The Economist*, American executive take-home pay relative to factory workers is considerably higher than in other nations. In Japan the average executive pay to average factory pay is 11 times greater, France 15 times, Canada 20 times, Britain 22 times, Mexico 47 times, and 475 times in the United States.

How Is Pay Set for a CEO?

The work of a CEO is often important to the success of a firm and one could argue as many do, there is a limited supply of CEO talent in America with high demand. What factors determine executive pay other than supply and demand and how does executive pay compare with firm performance?

Executive pay is generally determined by the board of directors that is often appointed by the CEO and approved by stockholders. Further, there is sometimes little relationship between CEO pay and the performance of the firm according to *Business Week*.

Is this an allocation by market or monopoly? You could easily argue either position; generally, for a given CEO, performance and conditions must be considered. CEO pay must ultimately be measured by his/her individual contribution margin to the firm.

Contribution Margin is the amount of value added to revenue by an input factor.

Factor Market is the exchange of factors from households to businesses including land, labor, capital, and entrepreneurship to business for rent, wages, interest, and profits respectively.

Marginal Factor Cost is the additional cost of one more factor inputs.

Marginal Productivity Theory is the theory that every input factor be paid according to its increase in value of output.

Marginal Revenue Product is the additional amount of value added to revenue by use of an input factor.

Net Effect is the net difference between the substitution and output effect.

Output Effect is the increase in output associated with decrease in costs of product and therefore, increases in demand for factor input.

Substitution Effect is the exchange between resource allocation of capital and labor dependent upon productivity between each factor input; there is a greater demand for input with greater productivity.

APPLIED EXERCISES:

EXERCISE 1 :

Betty owns a nail salon where customers are charged an average of $25 each. She can hire one worker for $110 per day including benefits. This first worker can serve six customers per day. Betty can hire a second worker who can serve five customers per day and a third worker who can serve four customers per day. If the cost of labor is purely competitive, and each additional worker can be hired for $110 per day, how many workers should Betty hire?

EXERCISE 2 :

Mark each of the following as True of False

_____ 1. The factor market is the market for goods by businesses.

_____ 2. The product market is the payment for land, labor, capital, and entrepreneurship.

_____ 3. Marginal productivity theory is the payment to resources according to their contribution to the value of their output.

_____ 4. The marginal factor cost (MFC) measures the additional cost of one more input resource.

_____ 5. The marginal revenue product (MRP) measures the revenue from the total of all inputs.

_____ 6. The equilibrium of a competitive labor market is the intercept of MFC = MRP.

_____ 7. Imperfect competition of labor resources equilibrium is less likely to hire more labor because the price drops with increases in output.

_____ 8. The output effect applies when the price of capital drops resulting in a decrease in resource costs and an increase in the number of workers.

_____ 9. The substitution effect applies to the change between capital and labor.

_____ 10. The income effect for individuals results in labor enjoying more leisure and doing less work.

APPLIED EXERCISES: ANSWERS

EXERCISE 1:

QUANTITY OF WORKERS	MARGINAL PRODUCT	MARGINAL REVENUE PRODUCT
1	6	$150
2	5	$125
3	4	$100

The MFC = $110 per day and the MRP = $125 @ two workers and $100 @ three workers. Therefore, only two workers should be hired.

EXERCISE 2:

False Questions: 1, 2, and 5

INTRODUCTION

International trade influences most institutions and individuals in the United States. Almost one of four jobs in America involves trade, and consumers purchase many imported products. Our trade impacts not only our nation but also our economic, political, and social relationships with other nations.

LEARNING OBJECTIVES

Please note the listed objectives. As you will see, the course materials are all objective driven.
This provides you with a constant way to direct and monitor your progress throughout the course.

1 OBJECTIVE ONE

Describe the role of global trade in the US economy.

2 OBJECTIVE TWO

Describe the roles of the US economy, the G8, the EU, and other trading blocks
in global trade.

3 OBJECTIVE THREE

Describe the basic concept of comparative advantage and give an example.

4 OBJECTIVE FOUR

Determine the gains of trade given production information for two countries in
production possibilities model.

5 OBJECTIVE FIVE

Discuss the dynamics of trade including the impacts of increased costs and trade
obstacles.

6 OBJECTIVE SIX

Discuss the benefits, costs, risks, and uncertainties of government trade barriers and
the case for open trade.

7 OBJECTIVE SEVEN

Describe the intensities of trade and the model of equilibrium in export and import
accounts.

THE IMPORTANCE OF GLOBAL TRADE TO THE UNITED STATES

The importance of the global market to the total American economy can be valued by comparing trade to the components of Gross Domestic Product (GDP), the market value of American expenditures.

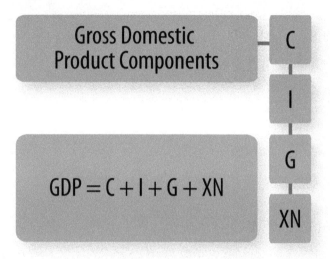

In the GDP model above, C is personal consumption expenditure, I is gross private domestic investments, G is total government expenditure, and Xn represents exports minus imports. The total American GDP was $17.4 trillion in 2014 and the Xn contributed a total of −$505 billion. The amount of exports was $2.3 trillion and the amount of imports was $2.8 trillion. Thus taken together imports + exports totaled almost $5 trillion of the $17.4 trillion gdp, accounting for 29% of the economy. Since imports were greater than exports, the net impact on gdp was a negative $505 billion. This imbalance is discussed in Lesson 13.

Since 1995, trade in both imports and exports has increased substantially and more than doubled as a percentage of GDP. The American percentage of total world trade is about 13%, falling from a historic high of 33% after World War II.

Trade is now more highly competitive than in previous decades because of technology and more open markets. New trade relationships with Asian nations have increased as a percent of total US imports from 3% in 1972 to over 23% today.

The United States is the largest nation in terms of GDP, the largest trade importer, and the second largest exporter in the world. China and Japan have GDPs at nearly equal levels and each have approximately half the GDP of the United States.

TABLE 12.1

Rank	Country	Exports	Imports	Total Trade	Percent of Total Trade
1	Canada	312	346.1	658.1	16.60%
2	China	124	466.7	590.7	14.90%
3	Mexico	240.3	294.2	534.5	13.50%
4	Japan	67	133.9	200.9	5.10%
5	Germany	49.4	123.2	172.6	4.30%
6	Korea, South	44.5	69.6	114.1	2.90%
7	United Kingdom	53.9	54	107.9	2.70%
8	France	31.2	47	78.2	2.00%
9	Brazil	42.4	30.3	72.8	1.80%
10	Taiwan	26.8	40.6	67.4	1.70%
11	India	21.6	45.2	66.9	1.70%
12	Saudi Arabia	18.7	47	65.7	1.70%
13	Netherlands	43.7	20.8	64.5	1.60%
14	Italy	17	42.1	59.1	1.50%
15	Belgium	34.8	20.9	55.7	1.40%

TABLE 12.2

	Output Before Trade	Output With Trade	Export + Import -	Output Avail. After Trade	Net Gain
England	5C	30C	−21C	9C	+4C
	9W	0W	+14W	14W	+5W
Portugal	20C	0C	+21C	21C	+1C
	10W	30W	−14W	16W	+6W

American Exports and Imports

America exports goods and services throughout the world but exports are concentrated with five nations: Canada receives 19% of total American exports, Mexico 15%, Japan 8%, China 8%, and United Kingdom 3%. American exports principally consist of agricultural products, 9 percent; chemicals, 27 percent; and capital goods (transistors, aircraft, computers, telecommunications equipment), 49%.

The American percentages of imports are also concentrated in five areas: European Union (EU 27 nations) 16%, Canada, 17%; China, 15%; Mexico, 14%; and Japan, 5%. The major imports include: agriculture, 5%; industrial supplies, 33%; capital goods, 30% (computers, telecommunications equipment); and consumer goods, 32% (automobiles, clothing, medicines, furniture, and toys).

Although the amount of American trade is about one fourth of the total American GDP, this trade is of critical importance. The products imported are essential to the functioning of American society and include such necessities as oil, computers, and automobiles. US oil imports are 3.9 million barrels per day down from 10 million but more than half of all automobiles purchased in the United States are produced by firms owned outside America.

The G8 Group

Global trade is largely dominated by industrially advanced nations. An international forum, the Group of Eight, consisting of the eight largest trading nations, meets annually to consider trade and global economic problems. The Group of Eight (G8) is composed of the United States, Japan, France, Germany, Italy, Canada, United Kingdom, and Russia. Some meetings include only the G7 excluding Russia. The European Union (27 member European nations) is also represented. The G8 nations constitute about 65% of global trade and together exercise an important influence on the world economy.

Trade has increased because of trading blocs that align nations into groups reducing barriers among member nations. Trading blocs are often referred to as free trade areas (FTAs).

The United States completed a free trade area (FTA) with Israel in 1985 and with Mexico and Canada in 1989. Within North America, the North American Free Trade Agreement (NAFTA) has decreased barriers and dramatically increased trade among Canada, the United States, and Mexico. A new imitative is currently underway in the United States to extend a FTA to other nations within Central and South America.

Within Europe, the European Union (EU) facilitates trade through a common market where there are few internal barriers and common external barriers. The members of APEC (Asia-Pacific Economic Cooperation) and OPEC (Organization of Petroleum Exporting Countries) are among the major trading nations establishing more cooperative trading relationships throughout the world.

Why Trade?

Because of the uneven distribution of resources among nations, there is economic advantage for nations to gain unavailable resources by exchanging for abundant resources. For example, the United States needs oil but has plentiful agricultural output; through exchange with OPEC nations, mutual benefit is gained.

Trade also provides benefits from economies of scale and labor specialization. Because of economies of scale, as higher output is produced for trade, average costs may decrease. In addition, nations specialize in labor that can be exchanged for economic benefit. Through increases in output sharing, there is a resulting decrease in production costs and an increase in the standard of living. For example, the United States imports electronics from Japan where economies of scale exist and Japan imports beef and chemicals from the United States where opportunity costs are less.

Basic Trade Theory

The analysis of trade is part of economic theory dating back to Adam Smith's publication of *An Inquiry into the Wealth of Nations* in 1776. Smith, the "Father of Economics," is noted for his insight into resource allocation. Smith was one of the first to use the relationships of trade to explain why some nations have an economic advantage. His major conclusion was that national economic well-being depends on the role of trade, competition, and limited government.

The theory of absolute advantage was the first economic model of beneficial trade. According to this theory, two nations should trade two goods if each nation is more efficient than the other in the production of one product; then each product can be exchanged for the other for mutual benefit. These relationships can be expressed algebraically and graphically for analysis.

The Basic Algebra of the Absolute Advantage Model

The output trade model measures output with a given input and uses production possibilities curves to graphically illustrate the cost/output relationship. The production possibilities model for a nation was discussed in Lesson 2.

These absolute advantage concepts can be applied in a simple example with only two nations and two products. Assume there are two trading nations, Alpha and Beta. Alpha using one unit of resource input can produce either two output units of X or one output unit of Y while Beta with the same inputs can produce either one unit of X or two units of Y, Figure 12.1. This is expressed algebraically within an equation by setting the x- and y-axis intercepts equal.

The algebraic equations are called cost ratios representing each nation with the maximum output of each of two products with a given input. Graphically these values are the intercepts of the production possibilities curves on the x- and y-axes. Each coefficient illustrates the maximum of a good that can be produced if only one product is made and none of the other. A higher coefficient represents greater efficiency (output per input).

FIGURE 12.1

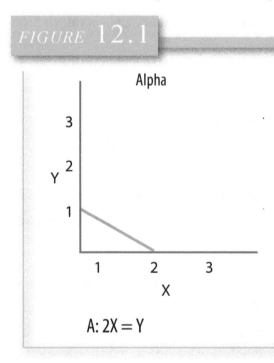

Alpha

A: 2X = Y

FIGURE 12.2

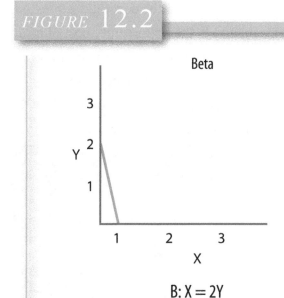

B: X = 2Y

Nation	X	Y		Nation	X	Y
Alpha	2	0		Beta	0	2
	0	1			1	0

Alpha: 2X = Y   Beta: X = 2Y

Absolute advantage exists in trade when one nation can produce more output of a product than another nation with the same input. In the cost ratio for Alpha and Beta above, Alpha has an absolute advantage in production of X because Alpha with one input unit can produce two of X and Beta with one input unit can only produce one X output unit. Beta has an absolute advantage in Y because Beta can produce two of Y with one input unit while Alpha can only produce one unit of Y with the same one unit of input. Therefore each nation has an absolute advantage in a different good, Alpha with X and Beta with Y.

In order to make trade beneficial to each nation, the trading possibilities (exchange of all possible trade combinations) must be to the right (larger) of the existing self sufficiency position (no trade). The trading possibilities line is the combination of possible trade outcomes with a given acceptable exchange rate. The cost ratio defines the output capabilities of a nation. However, to benefit from trade, the trade must result in a greater availability of goods or services than a nation has at self-sufficiency.

For trade to benefit each nation, the exchange must be within the limits of trade. The limits of trade are those initial cost ratio positions that each nation has at self-sufficiency expressed in terms of one variable. This is also the opportunity cost of producing one good compared to the other good for a given nation.

The limits of trade represent the lowest common denominator of the cost ratio expressed in the same good for each nation. The resulting equation is the opportunity cost of each good produced by a nation compared to the other good. Given the information above, for Alpha the opportunity cost of producing 1 unit of X is 1/2 unit of Y because $2X = Y$ (divide each side of the equation by 2). Beta must sacrifice 2 of Y to obtain 1 of X ($X=2Y$). The comparable limits of trade (opportunity cost) are shown below.

Cost Ratio:	**Alpha:**	**2X = Y**
	Beta:	**X = 2Y**
Limits of		
Trade:	**Alpha:**	**X = .5Y**
	Beta:	**X = 2Y**

> Trade must be within the trade limits to benefit each nation. The exchange of X must be less than 2Y but more than 1/2 Y ($2Y > X > 1/2Y$)

No Beneficial Trade

If the opportunity costs (limits of trade) are the same, neither nation can benefit from trade. The opportunity for trade is the comparability of possible benefits from the exchange of different cost ratios and if the cost ratios are the same, there is no benefit to share. An example of no trade could be:

Cost Ratio:	**Alpha:**	**2X = Y**
	Beta:	**4X = 2Y**
Limits of		
Trade:	**Alpha:**	**X = .5Y**
	Beta:	**X = .5Y**

In summary: The limits of trade are those initial cost ratio positions that a nation has at self-sufficiency and must be improved upon before trade will be beneficial.

The Terms of Trade

The terms of trade (also called exchange ratio) describe the units of goods given up for those goods received. The terms of trade must be within the limits of trade. The exact terms of trade are market derived and will depend on the value each nation places upon the items to be traded.

In the Alpha and Beta example, the terms of trade must be within the limits of trade, being more than the lower but less than the higher. In Alpha $2X = Y$ and Beta $X = 2Y$; therefore, the terms of trade must be greater than .5Y to X but less than 2Y to X. A market derived exchange ratio (term of trade) of X = Y would benefit each nation since 1X for 1Y is greater than 1/2Y but less than 2Y. Therefore the exchange ratio is within the limits: 2Y > X > 1/2Y.

Comparative Advantage

Trade theory evolved based upon the two nations/two products model. David Ricardo further developed the trade theory by advancing the theory of comparative advantage. His theory argues that two nations could benefit from trade as long as one nation did not have the same cost ratio (opportunity cost) as the other. Therefore, one nation could be more efficient at both goods exchanged but that nation should produce only the item that they are comparatively more efficient at producing (lower opportunity cost).

If both cost ratio coefficients are higher within one nation than the other nation, and the opportunity costs of each nation are different, then a comparative advantage exists in the nation with the higher coefficients. The more efficient nation has an absolute advantage in both products. To determine the maximum benefit from trade, the nation with the comparative (greater) advantage in one good would produce that good and the other good would be produced by the other nation.

The concepts of comparative advantage are applied below to nation A and nation B.

Cost Ratio:	**Nation A:**	**2X = 6Y**
	Nation B:	**X = 4Y**
Limits of Trade:	**Nation A:**	**X = 3Y**
	Nation B:	**X = 4Y**

Since the limits of trade differ, trade can be beneficial if the terms are: 3Y > X > 4Y.

Nation A has a higher coefficient for both X and Y since 2X > 1X (twice the efficiency by nation A in X) and 6Y > 4Y (1.5 times the efficiency by A in Y).

Since the limits to trade differ, the two nations can benefit from trade. Each nation should produce the good it has a greater comparative advantage or least comparative disadvantage in producing. Comparing the coefficients of the cost ratio for nation A to nation B relative to product X the ratio 2/1 = (2) is greater than the ratio relative to product

Y 6/4 = (1.5); therefore nation A should export product X and nation B should export product Y. Nation A is better at producing both goods, but has a comparative advantage in the production of product X.

Nation's Gain From Trade

Now we can apply our theory of trade to find the net benefits a nation gains from trade compared to no trade. Assume as a further application of two nations/two products trade theory that England and Portugal produce both wine and cloth. At self-sufficiency producing only one product, England can produce 30 of cloth (C) or 10 of wine (W) with the same of resource inputs. Portugal can produce 30 of cloth or 30 of wine with the same input resources. Self-sufficiency for each nation is shown in the production possibilities curves in Figures 12.3 and 12.4.

Cost Ratio: **England:**   **30C = 10W**
                         Portugal: **30C = 30W**

Limits of
Trade: **England:**   **3C = W**
                         Portugal: **C = W**

FIGURE 12.3

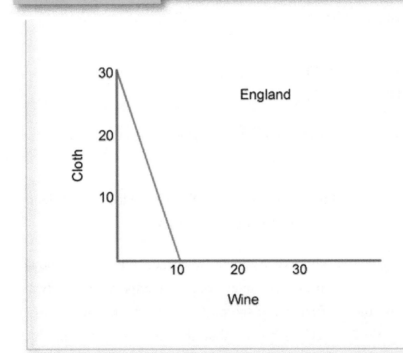

ENGLAND'S LIMITS OF TRADE IN PRODUCING WINE AND CLOTH

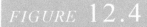

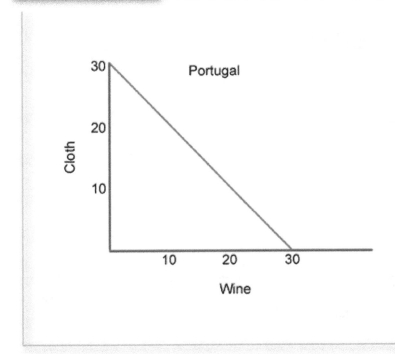

PORTUGAL'S LIMITS OF TRADE IN PRODUCING WINE AND CLOTH

From the limits of trade (or opportunity costs) shown, Portugal can produce three times (30/10) as much wine with equal input as England but each has equal output efficiency in cloth. Because the limits of trade differ, trade can be beneficial if the terms of trade are within the limits 3 C > 1 W > 1 C (terms must be greater than 1 C to 1 W but less than 3 C to 1 W).

Portugal has an absolute advantage in wine and England has a comparative advantage in cloth (England has equal advantage in cloth). Portugal should produce 30 wine and England should produce 30 cloth and each can benefit from trade if the terms of trade are within the limits of trade since the limits of trade are different.

FIGURE 12.5

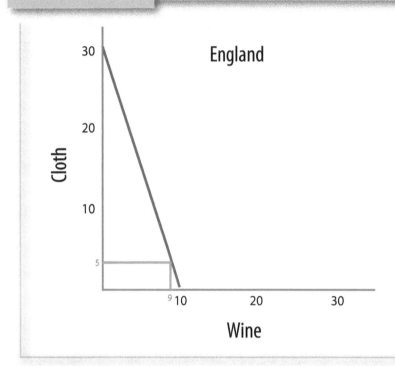

ENGLAND'S SELF-SUFFICIENCY PRODUCTION POSSIBILITIES

FIGURE 12.6

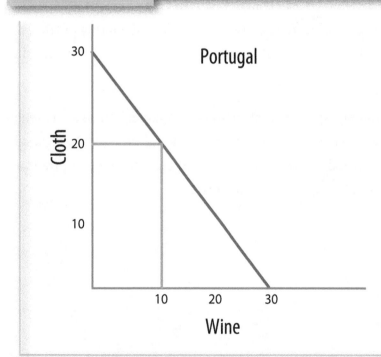

PORTUGAL'S SELF-SUFFICIENCY PRODUCTION POSSIBILITIES

The Trading Possibilities Line

If the market terms of trade (exchange ratio) are given as $30C = 20W$ then the terms are within the limits of trade $3C > 1W > 1C$. Dividing each side of the terms of trade by 10 results in $3C = 2W$ or $W = 1.5\ C$; this is within the limits of trade ($3C > 1W > 1C$). Using this information the trading possibilities line can be found illustrating all possible beneficial trade.

The advantaged trade position for each nation is found on the x- and y-axes of the graph. The maximum export output is the "anchor" for the trading possibilities line. As noted above, England will export 30 of cloth and Portugal will export 30 of wine. Therefore, the graph for England will intersect the y-axis (cloth) at 30 units and for Portugal the x-axis (wine) will intersect at 30.

The alternative axis for each nation is found by substituting into the equation of exchange (terms of trade). If the terms of trade are $30C = 20W$, and if England exports $30C$, England will get back 20 of W as noted in Figure 12.7. The anchor point and the 20W are next connected.

For Portugal, if 30W are exported and given the terms of trade: $30C = 20W$ (since $1W = 1.5C$ then $30W = 45C$ (1.5 times 30). The anchor point for Portugal of 30W is connected to 45C to form the trading possibilities line.

If Portugal sends out 30W, it will get back 45C. If England exports 30 of C, it will get back 20 of wine since $30C = 20W$. Notice the violet area is the trading possibility for each nation representing the possible benefits from trade.

The trading possibilities line illustrates all possible beneficial trade

ENGLAND'S TRADING POSSIBILITIES LINES

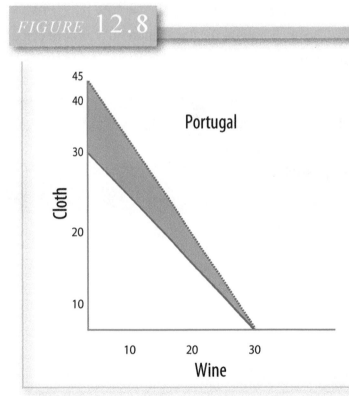

PORTUGAL'S TRADING POSSIBILITIES LINES

Nations Gains From Trade Matrix

The gains from trade matrix can be constructed if imports/exports are also given. See table below. If England decides to consume 14W, the net gain can be determined for each nation. Notice in the output before, column 1, the values relate to self-sufficiency with no trade (see Figures 12.5 and 12.6). Next, column 2, is the output with trade position where each nation specializes with comparative advantage. The export/import values, column 3, are derived from the given that England will consume 14W; therefore, with the terms of trade 30C = 20W (1.5C = W), the cost of importing 14 of W will be 21 of C (1.5 × 14 = 21). Exports from Portugal are imports to England. The output available after trade, column 4, is the output with trade (column 2) minus exports + imports (column 3) resulting in output available after trade. The net gain column, 5, is the comparison of column 1 (no trade) subtracted from output after trade (column 4).

TABLE 12.3

	Output Before	Output with Trade	Export + Import –	Output Avail. after Trade	Net Gain
England	5C	30C	–21C	9C	+4C
	9W	0W	+14W	14W	+5W
Portugal	20C	0C	+21C	21C	+1C
	10W	30W	–14W	16W	+6W

Analysis of the above relationships provides a check of the values. The two nations without trade together will have 5C + 20C but will have 30C from England with trade, the total gain of C will be 5C divided among both nations. In the table above net gain for England is 4C and Portugal is 1C validating the total gain of 5C.

For W, with no trade there would be 9W + 10W totaling 19 W but having 30 from Portugal with trade resulting in total gain of 11W (30-19). England obtains a gain of 5W and Portugal obtains a gain of 6W for a total of 11W; again confirming the total gain for both nations of 11W.

The conclusion is that each nation can gain by trade and thus have more goods available with trade than through self-sufficiency. Nations must not have the same cost ratio and the terms of trade must be within the limits of trade to benefit from trade.

The Dynamics of Trade

The exchange of goods and services within the global community is highly dynamic. New markets emerge and old production methods improve with new efficiencies. For the United States, growth in export trade will continue in areas such as medical technology and medical services, medications, entertainment, and legal and computer technologies.

The Law of Increasing Costs in Trade

As one nation increases output for export, the costs eventually begin to increase because of the law of increasing cost. The costs of production increase as a nation increases production quantity because the most efficient input resources are used first and then less efficient input resources must be employed. As costs increase, other nations have the opportunity to export that item because their costs will be comparatively less. Thus specialization is incomplete for a nation with any export because their cost advantage will eventually disappear.

Costs of Trade

If trade is beneficial, what possible reasons exist for trade restrictions? Beneficial trade requires conformity to the laws of economics. In order to be benefited by trade a nation must dynamically adjust to market needs and efficiencies. Within this context, some individuals do lose jobs and some firms do lose markets. Also, there is an opportunity cost of interdependency

> What possible reasons exist for trade restrictions?

through trade. When one nation trades with another nation, interdependency develops in terms of economics but also in the ability to be fully independent politically.

Trade Obstacles

Each trading nation has a unique culture that defines the social system. World trade challenges these differences by requiring communication and conformity to economic principles. For example, business practices are widely varied among America, China, and Saudi Arabia, but a vast amount of trade exists among these nations. A sensitivity to each culture is a necessity; however, it is also required that commerce take place within an efficient market.

The existence of monetary differences with constant currency value changes complicate trade exchanges. This dynamism is a necessary part of international trade but is a barrier to trade especially when contracts evolve over an extended period of time. Currency exchange risks can be shifted to financial sources but at a cost.

A final significant barrier to trade is government controls. In order to protect domestic markets, many governments construct trade barriers through tariffs, quotas, licenses, and non-tariff barriers. The benefits of trade are lessened or lost by barriers.

Government Trade Barriers

Trade restrictions take many forms but the most widely used are tariffs (tax on imports, seldom on exports). Protective tariffs are taxes imposed on imported goods that a nation is relatively less efficient in producing. The protective tariff increases prices to consumers but results in more inefficient domestic production, violating the benefits of trade. In some developing nations tariffs are often high in relation to the cost of the product—making the imported good largely unavailable.

Quotas are a limit set on the quantity of goods/services that can be imported into a nation. Quotas can be more limiting than tariffs because they set an absolute limit on imports. Until recently the United States and European nations had a quota on clothing imported from China and Argentine beef.

An embargo is a prohibition on importing or exporting goods or services from or to a nation. The United States has an embargo on trade with Cuba. An embargo is imposed for political reasons but does have an economic impact on global trade.

Non-tariff barriers (NTB) are varied types of barriers other than taxes. Some NTBs are applied to anti-dumping (dumping is selling below cost of manufacturing) rules and manufacturing requirements. NTB examples in the European Union include barriers to

> Monetary differences complicate trade exchanges

genetically modified organisms or beef injected with growth hormones. Tariff barriers have decreased globally through the World Trade Organization Agreement but some nations resort to NTBs to restrict trade. NTBs are often applied in the name of health concerns. Nations are able to slow or restrict trade through a NTB such as requiring costly box-by-box inspection of produce goods.

Why Do Trade Barriers Exist?

Developing nations (nations that are not highly industrialized) have a small economic base and are sometimes prone to protect their products or services. The loss of manufacturing or agricultural production might drastically impact the entire nation. These protected areas of the economy are highly visible for a nation and are thereby protected by politicians from competition.

A major reason for trade barriers in large industrialized nations is due to special interest groups that have political ties. Businesses seek protection in order to gain monopoly power and avoid competition.

A final reason trade barriers exist is the presence of political tensions. Economic barriers are constructed in order to provide political influences. This restriction is costly to consumers seeking a lower cost of living, unavailable local resources, and higher quality products and services.

Pro-Barrier Arguments

There are numerous arguments for restricting trade. Some of the more frequently advanced arguments include the following.

Military self-sufficiency suggests a nation must restrict trade to prevent other nations from acquiring a military advantage. This is a political argument and is not economic in nature.

The **domestic employment argument** suggests that trade decreases job opportunities in the importing nation. In practice, imports both eliminate and create jobs. Economists do not agree that trade only benefits exporters.

The argument that trade barriers **protect a domestic standard of living** suggests that trade barriers protect jobs. However, real wages (wages adjusted for currency value and inflation) are determined largely by productivity (output per worker-hour). Economic growth results from efficiency in producing globally desired goods and not because of restrictions.

The only economically acceptable reason for trade barriers is the **infant industry argument**. This argument suggests that temporary protection may be economically justified for a short period of time if a new industry is just beginning and would be destroyed by international competition.

Direct Effects of Tariffs

Trade barriers in general have the following impact:

- Increase domestic production but increase prices resulting in a decrease in domestic consumption.
- Misallocate resources domestically away from efficient production. Nations can benefit from trade with more efficient producers.
- Harm foreign producers who are efficient but provide domestic governments with increased revenue through tariffs.

Economic Indirect Impact of Free Trade

Most economists believe free trade keeps a nation's producers competitive and innovative while at the same time reduces prices and increases consumer well-being.

Costs of Protectionism (Trade Barriers)

Many studies have been completed on the costs/benefits of trade barriers. Some Americans seek to protect American jobs—but at what cost? The "benefits" of protectionism include keeping workers employed who are inefficient as well as providing revenue for a nation through tariffs. These benefits are estimated to be considerably less than the actual cost to consumers through price increases. The costs and benefits vary widely by industry according to economic studies but one study in 1984 estimated that consumers paid $42,000 annually for every textile job "saved."

Steel trade restrictions imposed by President Bush in 2000 were costly for consumers when tariffs were increased from 8% to 30%. According to the Mackinac Center for Public Policy, this tariff cost American consumers over $400,000 per job saved and actually resulted in a loss in other jobs (eight jobs lost for every job saved) due to price increases spread throughout the economy. This study is available at the Mackinac Center for Public Policy.

Intensities of Trade

A nation has an advantage or disadvantage in trade relative to each factor of production: land, labor, capital, entrepreneurship. The United States has intensity of trade in land products such as grains; capital intensity in production of medical equipment, computers, and chemicals; labor intensity in specialized areas of labor such as medical services; and entrepreneurship intensity with some small businesses operations. China has intensity in land, labor, and recently in capital production. Japan has intensity in skilled labor and capital in manufacturing of automobiles.

Equilibrium World Price, Exports, and Imports

A nation's export supply curve shows the quantities of a product it will export at world prices that exceed the domestic price—the price in a closed, no-trade economy. A nation's import demand curve reveals the quantities of a product a nation will import at world prices below the domestic price. In a two-nation model, the equilibrium quantities of exports and imports occur where one nation's import supply curve intersects the other nation's export demand curve.

Conclusion

Global trade creates more competition in world markets and as a result consumers have more choices of goods/services and lower prices. There are both positive and negative consequences from global trade for a nation. American industries with comparative advantage gain exports but industries with a comparative disadvantage lose their markets to more efficient global producers.

There are intervening economic consequences to the efficiency of global markets. The comparative advantage process does not consider the impact trade has on cultures or environment. No measure is made of negative sacrifices made by individual workers because of firms driven to cut costs. National laws vary widely on worker rights and there is no international norm that is guaranteed.

There are opportunities for workers, firms, institutions, and consumers to share in global trade benefits. However, national leaders must ensure viability of economic gain to be a positive global force without major negative spillover costs.

REAL WORLD ECONOMICS

HELP OR HINDERANCE? WHICH IS FREE TRADE?

One of the most controversial economic/political issues today is free trade. Free trade is generally defined as trade between nations without restrictions. Proponents argue that having free trade will promote better global efficiency of resource use. The result of such efficiency, proponents argue, will be lower costs and provide a higher standard of living throughout the world.

These economic positions have long been the conclusion of most economists, but is there a logical contrary position? The following arguments provide a counterview.

- As distribution systems become global, the greater wealth produced often accrues mainly to wealthy corporate owners and increases inequity in the world.

- In the United States, manufacturing jobs have been lost to service sector jobs, resulting in decreases in pay.

- Outsourcing of jobs from America have resulted in lower environmental and labor standards; some economists have referred to this process as a "race to the bottom."

- National security is lessened by a nation becoming dependent upon other nations for goods and services.

- Goods and services must travel longer distances resulting in more energy use and pollution.

The pro or con position of individuals often depends upon their relative position: am I gaining or losing from globalization? One can argue the merits or demerits of trade but one conclusion is certain: the process will continue and each worker must prepare himself for a global economy. The process cannot be ended but only modified for individuals according to skill and resource efficiency.

Group of Eight (G8) is a group of the eight largest trading nations meeting annually on trade and economic issues; nations include the United States, Japan, England, Canada, Italy, France, Germany, and the Russian Federation.

NAFTA: North Atlantic Free Trade Association is a free trade area including the United States, Mexico, and Canada.

Absolute Advantage occurs when a nation has greater efficiency (more output with a given input) in producing a good compared to another nation.

Cost Ratio is a resource output with a given input between two goods often expressed algebraically as equality between the x- and y-axis of a production possibilities curve.

Limits of Trade is an opportunity cost of a nation producing one product compared to another product, sacrificing one product to produce another product.

Comparative Advantage is beneficial trade when one nation has a greater output to input of two products than another nation, but more efficiency in one product than the other assuming different limits to trade.

Law of Increasing Cost in Trade is where costs of production increase as a nation increases production quantity of a good because the most efficient input resources are used first and less efficient input resources must be employed with increased output.

Tariff is a tax on imported good/service.

Quota is a limit on quantity of imported good from a given nation.

Embargo is a law prohibiting trade with another nation.

NTB: Non-tariff barrier restricts imports through means other than tariffs such as health standards or licensing of import goods.

Intensities of Trade is a specialization in a factor of production (land, labor, capital, entrepreneurship) by one nation compared to other nations.

APPLIED EXERCISES

EXERCISE 1 :

Mark each of the following True/False

_____ 1. Exports of goods and services from the United States make up 13% of GDP.

_____ 2. The United States exports a larger percentage of its GDP than most developed nations.

_____ 3. The United States is the largest exporter and importer with about 2% of total trade.

_____ 4. Since 1975, US exports have doubled as a percentage of GDP.

_____ 5. The United States currently exports more than it imports.

_____ 6. Trade reduces a nation's standard of living.

_____ 7. Capital-intensive goods for export include grains and beef.

_____ 8. The United States exports labor-intensive goods such as digital cameras.

_____ 9. Nations trade because of different resource endowments and labor specialization.

_____ 10. Nations can benefit from trading two items even if one nation is more efficient in production of both goods.

_____ 11. The limits of trade represent the domestic opportunity cost for a nation of producing two goods.

_____ 12. The cost ratio for a nation is the X- and Y-axes of the production possibilities curve.

_____ 13. The terms of trade represent how much of one product will be traded for how much of another as determined by the market.

_____ 14. The terms of trade must be within the limits of trade to be beneficial.

_____ 15. Because of increasing costs, specialization is seldom complete for a nation.

_____ 16. Free trade means not having trade restrictions.

_____ 17. Economists favor trade restrictions for most nations.

_____ 18. NTBs cause a nation to have a higher standard of living.

_____ 19. Tariff barriers benefit consumers.

_____ 20. Tariff barriers benefit inefficient domestic producers.

EXERCISE 2:

With the production possibilities curves below for Nation A and Nation B, what is the cost ratio for each? Could they benefit from trade? How would they trade?

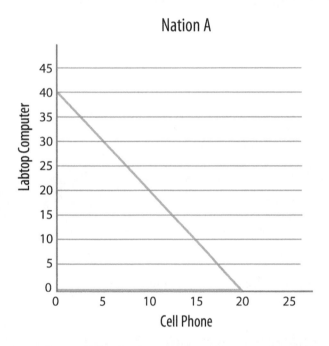

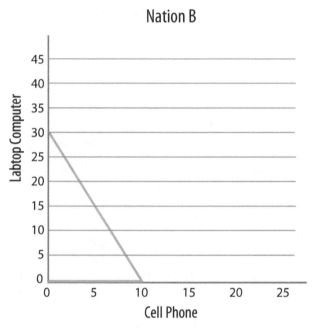

APPLIED EXERCISES: ANSWERS

EXERCISE 1 :

False statements: #3, 5, 6, 7, 8, 17, 18, 19

EXERCISE 2 :

The cost ratio for Nation A is: 20 CP = 40 LP and for Nation B is: 10 CP = 30 LC.

The limits to trade are:

CP = 2 LP and

CP = 3 LP;

Therefore the limits are different so each can benefit from trade.

The exchange ratio must be greater than one CP to one LP but must be less than one CP to 3LP. 3LP>CP>LP

Nation A is more efficient at each but has comparative advantage in CP. Nation A should export CP and Nation B should export LC.

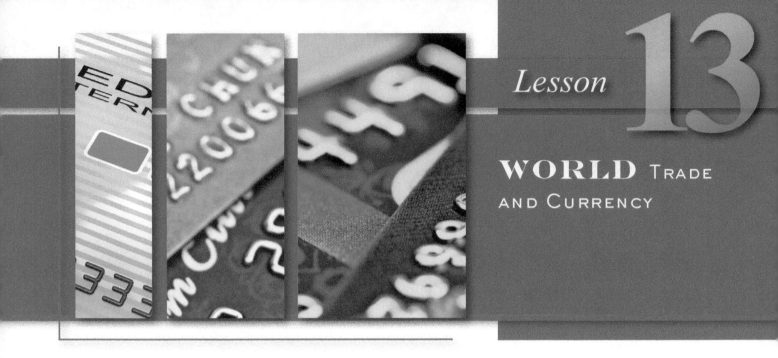

INTRODUCTION

Trade has been an important part of the American economy throughout history. In the early colonial period, tariffs were a major source of government revenue and this continued into early American history.

LEARNING OBJECTIVES

Please note the listed objectives. As you will see, the course materials are all objective driven. This provides you with a constant way to direct and monitor your progress throughout the course.

1 OBJECTIVE ONE

Provide a brief history of US trade with the rest of the world over the last 200 years including Civil War period.

2 OBJECTIVE TWO

Describe the recent structure of world trade organizations including the IMF, the World Bank, and the WTO.

3 OBJECTIVE THREE

Describe the process of financing international trade with an emphasis on currency values and balance of payment statement.

4 OBJECTIVE FOUR

Describe the role of flexible vs. fixed exchange rates.

5 OBJECTIVE FIVE

Interpret an example of supply and demand based on an exchange rate model.

6 OBJECTIVE SIX

Discuss the determinants of flexible exchange rate values.

7 OBJECTIVE SEVEN

Discuss the impacts of a negative balance of payments situation and the impacts of a trade deficit.

The Early American History of Trade

Tariffs were raised during times of war and depression resulting in magnified business cycles. United States tariffs were increased from 15% to 45% on merchandise imports during the Civil War (1860s). High tariffs ended when the federal government levied income taxes with the passage of the 16th Amendment to the Constitution in 1913.

Tariffs were again increased as the Depression began. The **Smoot-Hawley Tariff Act** in 1930 increased tariffs from 5% to 25% "to protect American businesses." However, over 60 nations trading with America quickly retaliated and this resulted in a fall in US trade by over 25%. Most economists believe these increased tariffs contributed to the depth and length of the Depression.

Trade History after the Great Depression

America began to revise tariff policies in 1934 with a newly elected Congress and President. The **Reciprocal Trade Agreement Act** was enacted giving the President the right to negotiate bilateral trade reductions. Between 1934 and 1945, American Presidents reduced tariffs with 32 nations from 25% to 5% as a percentage of merchandise imports.

Tariff rates then rose to 7% in the 1960s but again fell until 1985 when rates averaged less than 4%. Negotiations among global trade agencies caused tariff rates to fall throughout the 1990s and finally recorded an all time low of currently 1.3%.

World Trade Institutions

After global war and depression in the 1930s and 1940s, several institutions were established to facilitate economic growth and trade. The most successful initiative occurred at the conclusion of World War II in 1944 through the United Nations "Nations Monetary and Financial Convention." Forty-four nations met at Bretton Woods, New Hampshire to form an agreement creating new institutions for economic stability. The location namesake, The Bretton Woods Agreement, was completed to avoid exchange rate disequilibrium, reduce trade barriers, and facilitate economic recovery.

> The confrence at Brentton Woods, representing nearly all the peoples of the world has . . .

The Bretton Woods Agreement

To facilitate post war reconstruction, the **Bretton Woods Agreement** created a new international monetary institution called the International Monetary Fund to stabilize exchange rates. When member nations maintained their currency value of exchange with a small percentage called a band, this nation could borrow from the IMF for temporary stabilization. Currency rates were fixed within a parity zone to the US dollar or with the IMF.

The Bretton Woods Agreement also created the International Bank for Reconstruction and Development, known as the **World Bank**, to facilitate postwar reconstruction.

The IMF and the World Bank promoted economic stability and reconstruction of Europe after World War II. The IMF system of defined parities between local currencies with the US dollar or IMF was used from 1946 until 1970. The World Bank continues to fund global economic development. The Bretton Woods system of parities operated effectively until 1970. However, at that time deficits in payments would have forced the United States to relinquish much of its monetary gold so the United States began valuing the dollar on a managed floating rate and many other nations followed. The value of major trading nations' currencies became largely set by market forces of supply and demand.

The International Trade Organization and the General Agreement on Tariffs and Trade (GATT)

A final element of the Bretton Woods Agreement proposed the International Trade Organization (ITO) to reduce trade barriers and settle trade disputes. This organization was not approved by the US Congress, but a similar initiative was accepted three years later (1947) with the creation of The General Agreement on Tariffs and Trade (GATT). The GATT agreement was signed initially by 23 nations but later grew to include over 100 nations.

> . . . considered matters of international money finance which are important for peace and prosperity

A review of the Bretton Woods Agreement can be found at: http://go.worldbank.org/A5PNZYX5T0. This site describes the development of the Bretton Woods Agreement as well as the impact of building a new international monetary system.

The World Trade Organization (WTO)

GATT was reorganized into the World Trade Organization in 1995. The goal of the WTO is to facilitate free trade without "undesirable side-effects." According to the WTO agreement the trading system should be:

Without Discrimination

A country should not discriminate between its trading partners (giving them equally "most favored nation status") and it should not discriminate between its own and foreign products, services or nationals.

More Free

Barriers should come down through negotiation.

Predictable

Foreign companies, investors, and governments should be confident that trade barriers (including tariffs and non-tariff barriers) should not be raised arbitrarily and are bound by the WTO commitments.

More Competitive

Discouraging "unfair" practices such as export subsidies and dumping products at below cost to gain market share.

More Beneficial

For less developed counties—giving these nations more time to adjust, greater flexibility, and special privileges.

For more information on the WTO, visit: http://www.wto.org.

WTO: The Most-Favored-Nation Status and Dispute Resolution

Equal treatment of nations was embodied in the "most-favored-nation status" (MFN) of the WTO. Tariffs and other trade restrictions must be equal among all nations within the WTO, with no discrimination against any one nation.

Another important provision of the WTO agreement was the settlement of disputes. An established process allows any nation to file an appeal and explain their complaint. The WTO seeks to resolve such problems through negotiation.

WTO Conferences

Several trade negotiations (conferences) have taken place through GATT and the WTO to promote trade. **The Tokyo Round** (1973-1979) dealt with tariffs and non-tariff barriers. **The Uruguay Round** (1986-1994) dealt with intellectual property, textiles, agriculture and WTO rules. Negotiations have continued over many years including the **Doha Development Agenda** (2001–2013), the **Bali Round** (2013) and the **Nairobi Conference** of 2015. These discussions for over 13 years mainly contested of trade related agricultural subsidies and topics from technology transfer to economic development. A series of negotiations centered in Cancun (2003), Geneva (2004–2008), Paris (2005), and Potsdam (2007) have not be able to resolve issues. Critical issues are related to agriculture imports in developing nations where a majority of citizens derive their living from the land. Other issues also relate to patents on medications.

International institutions trying to promote trade have been challenged by charges that trade promotes substandard employee safety, wages, and global sustainability. Some people argue that increases in trade result in a "race to the bottom" where nations with the lowest standards gain advantage in lower cost production. This notion is however disputed by most economists who believe that over time, developing nations with growth gain in worker welfare and environmental sustainability.

Financing International Trade

Payments for trade must be made through exchanging one currency for another. In order to pay for imported goods or services the individual or firm must secure currency from the exporting nation (increasing demand for the export nation's currency) by supplying currency from the importing nation (increasing supply of the importing nation's currency). The international currency exchange process takes place through banks or exchange dealers.

The Value of Currency

Currency value is determined through either a flexible or fixed exchange system. The United States has a flexible exchange rate system (variable rate) where the value of the dollar is determined through the forces of supply and demand within international markets.

Some nations, however, maintain a fixed exchange rate determining the value of their currency relative to a key currency (such as the US dollar, group of currencies, or gold).

Trade and the Value of Currency

American exports partially pay for American imports. The demand for American products or services creates a demand for US dollars and American imports create a supply of dollars. US imports tend to move in tandem with US exports (Figure 13.1). A Japanese firm importing American beef must exchange Japanese yen for the American dollar to make payment, while an American firm importing Japanese automobiles must exchange dollars to make payment in yen. These global economic payments are categorized and measured within the balance of payments statement.

FIGURE 13.1

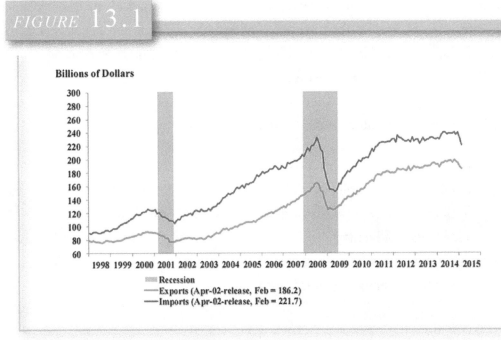

US IMPORTS AND EXPORTS

From http://www.dallasfed.org. Copyright © by Federal Reserve Bank of Dallas. Reprinted by permission.

The Balance of Payments Statement

The **Balance of Payments Statement** is a summary of all economic transactions of a nation much like a national income statement accounting for global transactions. For the US current balance of payments information, go to the site below. http://www BOPIIP.bea.gov/international/ai1.htm#

The US Balance of Payments, 2014 (in billions)

Current Account	
US goods exports	$1,635
US goods import	−2,371
Balance on goods	−736
US exports of services	710
US imports of services	−479
Balance on services	231
Balance on goods and services	−505
Net investment	450
Net transfers	−58
Balance on investment income and transfers	392
Balance on current account	−113
Capital and financial	
Balance on capital/financial account	77
Estimated errors and omissions	36
Balance of payments account	0

Payment transactions are recorded through a double-entry accounting system. The balance of payments must always balance just as any double-entry accounting statement. Within a balance of payments statement, inflows of funds to a nation are recorded as a credit (+) and outflows are recorded as a debit (-). Notice in the statement above that each entry with a positive value brings funds into the United States and each entry with a negative value sends funds outside the United States. Exports are positive and imports are negative.

The Current Account of the Balance of Payments

The current account section of the statement includes imports and exports, services, net investment income, and net transfers (gifts exchanged by individuals or private groups).

Currently, most current accounts are in deficit except investment income. Americans are now buying more goods and services abroad than they are selling. Net transfers are private donations or pensions sent to those outside the United States.

The balance on the 2014 current account was a $–113 billion. This disequilibrium required a balancing payment from the capital and financial accounts. As Americans buy more goods and services than they sell and give more gifts, net investment inflow is not sufficient to cover the other current account outflows. The payments balance is secured from purchases of United States assets such as United States Treasury bills, bonds, and notes as well as the sale of American businesses and land to international investors. Official settlements balances can also be used if available to offset deficits.

The United States Balance of Payments and Official Settlements Balance

US Official Settlements Balance is the accounting for reserves of other nations' currencies held by the US central bank (the Federal Reserve) from previous payments surpluses.

Demand is determined by the sovereign (indepentent) consumer

Central banks of a nation hold reserves as well as balances with the International Monetary Fund that can be drawn upon for balancing short-term balance of payment deficits.

Flexible Exchange Rates Equilibrium Process

Within flexible exchange rate systems, each trading nation's currency is valued by the supply and demand for their currency. For example, if the United States is importing more goods and services from Canada, this difference in balance must be paid by US dollar outflow. With an increase in Canadian exports to America, the demand for the Canadian dollar will increase and the supply of American dollars will also increase in the international currency market. Notice in Figure 13.2, the supply line of Canadian dollars remains constant but the demand for Canadian dollars increases from D1 to D2 resulting in an appreciation of the Canadian dollar compared to the American dollar. Within the United States the demand for dollars remains constant but the supply of American dollars increases from S1 to S2 within the international market resulting in a decrease in the value of the American dollar, Figure 13.3.

FIGURE 13.2

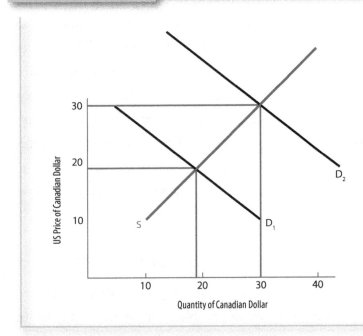

VALUE OF CANADIAN DOLLAR

FIGURE 13.3

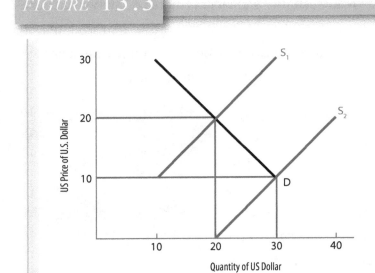

VALUE OF US DOLLAR

Fixed Exchange Rates

Some nations maintain a fixed currency exchange system in order to control the value of their currency at a constant rate of exchange among currencies. These nations make internal adjustments to bring equilibrium to their balance of payments. When major disequilibrium occurs, the nation is either forced to change currency value or adjust their economy relative to trade. A nation may change value by devaluing their currency, decreasing the value compared to other currencies/gold or re-valuing its currency, increasing the value compared to other key currencies/gold. For a review of this process and the history of currency valuation, read: The Federal Reserve of New York Website, FEDPOINT, (Currency Devaluation and Revaluation). http://www.newyorkfed.org/aboutthefed/fedpoint/fed38.html

Flexible Exchange Rates and Fixed Exchange Rates

Both flexible and fixed exchange rate systems work well as long as a nation's balance of payments remains substantially in balance. However, problems arise when the balance of payments of a nation becomes in disequilibrium with either a surplus or a deficit, but especially with a deficit. There are advantages and disadvantages of each currency exchange system to adjust for disequilibrium.

Fixed exchange rates do provide greater stability and there is more certainty of currency value for business contracts. Contracts can be written with relative assurance that the value of the currency will remain the same (fixed). A nation with a fixed exchange system must maintain the economy to continue a constant exchange rate.

The value of the currency can be influenced by a government in a payments deficit. Central banks can use past currency official reserves (past surpluses) if they are available. Otherwise, restrictions are imposed to reduce imports, or other measures are taken domestically to balance exports and imports. A recession within a nation will reduce imports directly but the impact on

> A recession within a nation will reduce imports directly

the national economy is negative. Other means of reducing merchandise deficits include reducing inflation or imposing exchange controls matching export payments with import payments. These methods are costly to a nation and reduce the benefits from trade.

Flexible exchange rates allow for an automatic adjustment of exchange value on a real-time basis. This system however makes contract costs scheduled for delivery in the distant future less certain. Either contracting party may be negatively impacted by the change in the value of currency. The actual cost of the good or service will be increased or decreased by the difference in exchange rates. Change in currency value can impact national inflation, employment, and income.

Determinants of Flexible Exchange Rates

Several variables influence flexible exchange rate currency value. All other things remaining the same, each of the following changes will depreciate or appreciate the value of currency compared to other currencies.

When **real interest rates** (nominal interest rates minus the inflation rate) are higher in nation A than nation B and all other things remain the same, the value of A's currency will increase. Higher real interest rates in nation A will induce nation B's investors to move B's currency to nation A to obtain a higher yield. The demand for A's currency will increase, appreciating the value of A's currency. The value of B's currency will increase in supply as it is converted to A's currency and this increase in supply will depreciate B's currency value.

The **relative income** of nations impacts currency value. Nations with increases in national income will have a higher demand for imports and thus increase the supply of their currency, depreciating the value of their currency. Nations with comparatively low growth will have a higher demand for exports and the value of their currency will appreciate.

The **relative inflation** rates between nations directly impacts prices and therefore trade. A nation with a higher inflation rate will buy more imports and sell fewer exports decreasing the value of their currency. A nation with a lower inflation rate will sell more products and increase the value of their currency.

Speculators also cause changes in the price of currency when they trade in turbulent markets. Speculators will buy or sell currency for temporary advantage and cause less stability in currency markets.

Finally, central banks sometimes use managed float to intervene directly into the global currency market to stabilize their currency. Central banks hold reserves of other nations' currencies and may purchase their own currency when value is falling, thereby increasing demand and value. Central banks may also sell their currency to lessen increases in their currency's value by increasing their currency supply. This process is also sometimes called "dirty float" because it is a direct government intervention in an otherwise free market.

Negative Current Account History

After World War II the United States maintained a positive current account in the balance of payments but had a negative balance in capital and financial accounts because of the financial and capital outflow of American dollars for reconstruction and investment in Europe and Japan.

Recently, however, most current account values except investment income are currency outflows and are balanced by inflows of international currency into the capital and financial accounts.

The negative values in the current account are due to:

- Higher relative growth in the United States compared to other nations, thereby increasing imports over exports.
- Decreases in trade barriers and emergence of volume imports from Asia.
- Large inflows in the capital account allowing Americans to reduce saving and buy more imports.

The United States has been a major growth engine for trade. Although Americans do have some trade restrictions; the United States has largely encouraged global trade. American imports allow other nations to have more dollars for global trade.

The recent influence of Asian trade is significant and dramatic. Beginning in 2005–2006, trade barriers on Asian goods fell and Asian imports of consumer goods such as clothing dramatically increased in European (EU) and US markets. With increased international exports, Asian nations such as China maintained a very large trade and balance of payments surplus with the US and EU.

American Current Account Deficits

Continued American deficits in the current accounts are a matter of concern. While there are varied views on the short-term consequences of this condition, there is widespread agreement that a continued negative trend would not be in America's best interest. When America depends on Europe and Asia for necessary savings for American investments, a growing dependency develops. European and Asian withdrawal of funds from the

United States would be a financial outflow creating a crisis or at the very least an American recession. Interest rates would necessarily be increased and the American economy would slow and experience inflation as well.

The American current trade deficit with China is about −$342 billion in 2014. China currently owns over $3 trillion in American investments. Past financial investment inflows by foreigners into the United States require annual American currency outflows for interest and profit payments.

American exports to China have not grown to match imports from China. There are several reasons for the growing deficit with China. Of course there is comparative advantage in China with many goods, however, with payments deficits in America, this should lead to increased valuation of the Chinese currency, the yuan. However, China has largely fixed the valuation of their currency to a group of large trading nations including the United States. With increases in demand for the yuan, but little or no increase in value relative to the dollar, the cost of Chinese imports do not adjust to a higher value but continue to be less expensive while American goods increase in price.

The yuan has increased in value by over 20 percent against the dollar since 2005 and this increase in value will continue as China seeks to reduce its inflation rate. However, further lessening will proceed at a lower rate in order to maximize exports/employment. China's current account surplus was 10 percent of global trade in 2007 but the surplus is now down to less than 3 percent in 2012.

The American trade deficit is also influenced by American oil purchases from abroad. Before 2007 oil imports continued to climb with increased US energy use causing large deficits in the trade accounts until recently. Beginning in 2011 and forecast to continue for 30 years (Slone Foundation Study, 2012), increases in oil and natural gas production have increased to a 15 year high and it is possible the United States will again be the major oil producer and perhaps even self-sufficient in energy within 5 years. Oil imports in 2013 are expected to be about 40 percent of consumption, down from over 60 percent in 2010. New oil and natural gas exploration technology has dramatically increased output and will continue to do so giving the United States a potential advantage in some areas. However, overall goods and services negative balances are significantly in deficit and expected to continue to exist.

Other nations may act to support the American economy in order to promote their own exports (jobs). There is much of an unknown element in this arrangement in the long term, however, and the result is much interdependency within the trading community. In the long run, America must establish equilibrium in outflow and inflow of payments.

The fragility of the American financial position was illustrated in 2008 by the sub-prime mortgage crisis starting in the United States and soon negatively impacting banks and investment institutions throughout the world. America and other governments were forced to support mortgage and credit markets to prevent a national or even global financial crisis. America will need to balance payments in the long run to restore confidence and maintain American economic independence.

CONCLUSION

The Long-Run Consequences of American Balance of Payments Deficits

While most economists agree the impact on America of short-run deficits are debatable, the long-term implications are more disquieting. In the short run the United States continues to consume more than it produces and the American current standard of living is benefited. Americans are able to have more goods/services available and are able to afford a higher level of consumption.

In the long run if continued deficits cause a loss of confidence in American investments, a financial crisis will result and funds will be withdrawn. As funds are withdrawn from America, a reduction in the value of the dollar will occur. The dollar has been losing value since 2001 as shown in Figure 13.4. A decrease in the value of the dollar brings inflationary pressure on the American economy as more dollars have to be spent for the same amount of goods. Many economists do not consider the balance of payments or the balance of trade deficits an immediate problem as the world also is benefited by American imports.

Balance of Payments Statement is a national income statement of currency inflow and outflow.

Current Account Balance is the balance of payments section measuring currency inflows and outflows in goods, services, investment income, and net transfer accounts.

Capital and financial accounts is the balance of payments section measuring foreign currency inflows and outflows of asset purchases including both real and financial assets.

Flexible exchange system is an international market system valuing currencies based on supply and demand.

Fixed exchange system is an exchange system where currency value is fixed relative to other currency, currencies, or gold.

Managed Float is a central bank intervention into flexible exchange market to stabilize their currency value.

Currency Appreciation is an increase in value of a currency within the international market.

Currency Depreciation is a decrease in value of a currency within the international market.

Smoot-Harley Tariff Act allowed for an increase in American tariffs to protect American jobs during the depression but resulted in retaliation by other nations matching tariffs and in trade losses.

WTO: World Trade Organization is the largest global trade institution promoting trade and economic development.

GATT: General Agreement on Tariffs and Trade was an international institution promoting international trade and was predecessor of the WTO.

MFN: Most-favored-nation status is part of WTO agreement seeking equal treatment of all participants to the agreement.

APPLIED EXERCISES

EXERCISE 1 :

Mark each of the following True/False

_____ 1. US exports create a demand for dollars in the exchange markets.

_____ 2. The balance of payments is the income statement for a nation.

_____ 3. Imports to a nation increase the supply of currency of that nation in exchange markets.

_____ 4. The current account of the balance of payments statement lists the balance of goods, services, investment income, and net transfer payments.

_____ 5. The United States has a positive balance of trade within the current account.

_____ 6. The United States has a net positive inflow of capital from other nations.

_____ 7. A trade deficit occurs when a nation exports more goods and services than it buys from other nations.

EXERCISE 2 :

Describe the influence on freely floating rates of a currency if each of the individual events occurs. Assume you are considering the impact on the English currency, the pound sterling.

A: Higher interest rates in England

B: Lower price level increases (rate of inflation) in England

C: The expectation that cell phones will be cheaper in the future.

D: Higher national income increases in England

E: Lower national income increases in England

APPLIED EXERCISES

EXERCISE 3 :

If a nation wishes to have a surplus in the balance of payments account, that nation would maintain a (high/low) value to its currency. This in turn would tend to (increase/decrease) its employment.

EXERCISE 4 :

A nation with a negative balance of payments and a negative balance of trade will tend (all other things remaining the same) to have (increasing/decreasing) value of its currency relative to other currencies.

APPLIED EXERCISES: ANSWERS

EXERCISE 1:

False statements: #5, 7.

EXERCISE 2:

A. **Higher interest rates in England**

Increase in demand for English currency, appreciates value

B. **Lower price level increases (rate of inflation) in England**

Increase in demand for English currency, appreciates value

C. **Higher national income increases in England**

Increase in imports increases supply of English currency in markets with a depreciation in value

D. **Lower national income increases in England will cause fewer imports to be purchased in England resulting in a decrease in England currency value with increases in the demand for English exports. This action in the longer term will increase the demand for English currency with an increase in the value of the English currency restoring the value.**

Increase in demand for exports, increases demand for English currency, appreciates value

EXERCISE 3:

If a nation wishes to have a surplus in the balance of payments account it would maintain a (high/low) value to its currency. This in turn would tend to increase its employment.

EXERCISE 4:

A nation with a negative balance of payments and a negative balance of trade will tend (all other things remaining the same) to have decreasing value of its currency relative to other currencies.